The Treasured Age

Spirituality for Seniors

James F. Finley, CSP

ALBA · HOUSE   NEW · YORK

SOCIETY OF ST. PAUL, 2187 VICTORY BLVD., STATEN ISLAND, NEW YORK 10314

Library of Congress Cataloging-in-Publication Data

Finley, James.
    The treasured age: spirituality for seniors / by James F. Finley.
        p.116   cm. 21 × 14
        ISBN 0-8189-0554-9
        1. Aged — Religious life.   I. Title.
    BV4580.F53   1989
    248.8'5—dc19   88-36695
                                                    CIP

Designed, printed and bound in the United States of
America by the Fathers and Brothers of the
Society of St. Paul, 2187 Victory Boulevard,
Staten Island, New York 10314, as part of their
communications apostolate.

Printing Information:

Current Printing - first digit   2 3 4 5 6 7 8 9 10 11 12 .

Year of Current Printing - first year shown
            1990   1991   1992   1993   1994   1995   1996

Contents

Introduction

When I mentioned to a young priest friend of mine who was visiting me that I was minded to do a book on spirituality for seniors, he commented bluntly and dryly: "Of all the unnecessary books written, yours may well top the list."

"Why?" I asked.

"Because when people get to the stage of being 'seniors,' it seems to me they either have a sense of the importance of God or they haven't. They show some sensibility to the need for spiritual values and development in their lives or they don't. And if they don't possess it, I would guess it's too late to do much about their lack."

He enjoyed the shock my face registered at his summary dismissal of my project. "What it comes down to is that by the time people have achieved senior citizen status, they have either learned to say their prayers or they haven't." He moved in to finish me off with a final rapier thrust. "Besides, it appears to be that most of the 'haves' feel they've got heaven made. The 'have nots' couldn't care less."

"You're much too young to be so cynical," I objected, as I pulled my notes toward me to indicate the project was dear to me and would continue.

"And you're much too old to be so naive," he countered,

as he left me — and left me, I must admit, with something of a doubt.

Is there an age, a stage, in the average good or pious person's maturing, when their reach to, search for, need of spiritual development comes to some limit? Do they have a temper, a mood, an attitude that justifies our young priest's comments? They have learned to pray and now in these late years of life, many of them feel they have heaven made. They have taken their souls about as far as they feel is needed. They are satisfied with their spiritual life.

In a dozen years as pastor of a parish where the elderly bulked large, I had never found such complacency in the seniors to whom I and my staff ministered. In many ways, they showed their awareness for the need to develop spiritually. They were the ones — not we priests — who wanted extra masses or devotions added to the parish schedule. They were the ones — not we priests — who resisted and resented any cutting back on times and opportunities for confessions. And, they were the ones — if a hospital confinement was approaching — who informed us well in advance that they expected to be brought the sacraments for the duration.

All the evidence from seniors themselves and from experts in the care of the elderly confirm this personal observation from parochial experience. Not only are seniors not complacent about their spirituality but they are highly critical of what they perceive to be neglect in having their spiritual needs attended to.

Many of them feel the churches are geared toward the young and take the elderly for granted. As one senior lady said in an article on the elderly and their spirituality, carried by the *National Catholic Register* a year back: "I don't feel as much a part of the church as I used to. They think you're too old and you've been a member so long that they don't need to do anything for you because you're just going to stick with it. They take you for granted. And so you feel that the church isn't interested in you."

In the same article, Monsignor Charles Fahey, who as director of the Third Age Center at Fordham University has worked with the problems of the elderly, corroborates this lady's observation. Monsignor Fahey remarked: "We do take older persons for granted." He believes that the elderly have special problems they should be assisted in handling. "Anyone who has lived through a lot of social change and suffered losses, both physically and socially, needs to integrate all this."

Monsignor Fahey admitted knowing many Catholics growing old in a normal fashion who feel spiritually removed from the Church. He says that their spirituality could be enhanced in a number of ways, from simply knowing their name to making Mass as accessible as possible and from targeting homilies to their older lives to developing a sense of community around the liturgy.

It would appear then that contrary to my young compatriot's curt dismissal of the worthwhileness of giving attention to seniors and their spirituality, there is an actual need for such an apostolate.

Believing this to be so, I have tried over the past few years since retirement, to provide some small spiritual assistance to the seniors of my acquaintance. I mail out a quarterly newsletter to them and always devote part of the letter to their spiritual growth and development.

The Treasured Age is a collection of these spiritual notes or meditations. They have been arranged according to some broad general themes which concern seniors, perhaps, a bit more pertinently than they do other age groups. True, no particular age group is ever free from concern over sickness and suffering, the need for virtue, or fears about death and dying. Seniors, however, are up a lot closer to some of these concerns than the younger generations.

I pray that these reflections may prove a benefit to all seniors who come upon them. Especially I pray they prove a benefit to those who are looking for that guidance that will help them to grow and develop spiritually. May these reflections help deepen that realization they have that no one is ever too old (as St. Richard of Chichester wrote) "to know God more clearly, love him more dearly, and follow him more nearly."

SECTION ONE

Our Attitude

Seniors who keep very busy, involved
Vibrantly active, I find,
Seem less concerned with the state of their health
But, more, with the state of their mind . . .

1 Old Age

I am tempted to leave this page blank with no more on it than the title and the simple instruction: "Fill the page yourself." That is how personal, individual, singular, particular, different, special and separate I believe each of us regards this state of old age. For each of us, there is a unique viewpoint and it is ours alone.

Notice, in beginning this reflection, I wrote "this state of old age." I didn't say "this state of being old." There is a difference and a distinction. The *state of old age* is something that happens to us because of the inexorable counting of the great clock of life. Seconds tick away, minutes mount up, hours pass, days end, only to be succeeded by another day that resumes the cycle of passing time and the process of aging for us and our world. The passing of years inevitably moves us and our world to an older stage of life.

The world and *everyone* in it — even the newest born infant — gets older at the same time. Senior citizens are not alone in aging, though you would think, as you listen to some of our elders that they are the only ones among us who age. But, as Walt Whitman warned the young:

> Youth, large, lusty, loving — Youth
> full of grace, force, fascination,
> Do you know that Old Age may come after you?

Simply, as night follows day and day, night, we all get old together. Old age is a happening and it happens to all.

The state of being old, on the other hand, is more under our control. We have more responsibility here, forestalling it, ignoring it, rejecting it. No matter what the calendar of years for us, we *refuse* to act our calendar age.

Permit me another quote from another great and very ancient writer, Cicero. (Quotations on old age, by the way, can be culled from the earliest of times to the present. Understandably, the subject has fascinated all peoples of all periods in man's history.) Cicero, who has written one of the most famous of books on old age, stated:

> For as I like a young man in whom there is something of the old, so do I like an old man in whom there is something of the young; and he who follows this maxim, in body will possibly be an old man, but he will never be an old man in mind.

Now do we see why I wanted to leave a blank page after I entered my title on this reflection? I wanted to help us find out what we, who may be listed as seniors, or as elders, or as old, have in *our* minds about this state of life.

We should see ourselves as able to make as much of a contribution to life as we ever did. Look at the Church, at government, business, sports, or at the entertainment world. Each shows seniors as not merely contributing to, but as managing huge enterprises. These seniors, who are leaders in the worlds they direct, have no consciousness that their advanced years mean they must forfeit vigor of life or curtail the involved activities in which they engage. These people are living contradictions to the concession too many seniors make when they say that life's activities and enterprises belong to the young.

In our own circles, our contribution can be made on the same high level. That *it is made*, that *it will be made*, depends on *how* we see ourselves. Do we have a negative image of ourselves that shows us as being old, or rather, do we view ourselves positively as merely being in an older age bracket?

In one of the paragraphs above, I did highlight the phrase "in our mind." I am well aware that with advanced years we cannot control the toll that age takes on our bodies. Aches, pains, ills, incapacitations of one sort or another are going to slow us down. They may be so severe that they may stop us in our tracks.

On average, however, they should not stop us in our minds. We can maintain mental activities at a level far above that which we might expect of ourselves or a level we imagine we are capable of. We can still be curious about our globe, read its books, study its problems, know its plans, chart its progress as it attempts to make a brave new world in which all God's children can work out their salvation.

One of the truest sayings ever uttered is: "We're only as old as we think we are." As an exercise in discovering our own attitude, we might try doing what I was tempted to ask we do at the beginning of this reflection. Take a blank sheet of paper and fill in our own thoughts under the title: Old Age.

The result would tell us how old we really think we are. And — if we find we think of ourselves as *being old* rather than just in the state of senior citizenship, we have a signal on the need to change our attitude immediately.

2   Past Is Past: Amen

Despite all the glowing copy written about the joys, glories, relaxations, and other such delights and benefits of retirement, I don't think there is any moment more traumatic for most than that instant when the shattering realization of the finality of retirement sinks in on us.

I well recall that instant when it occurred for me. I was driving away from the parish where I had served as pastor for the previous six years. My mind was reeling a little as it tried to manage the facts of retirement life that were forcing themselves into my consciousness. This part of my life is over. I am finished here. I am no longer pastor. The parish will go on. *I am no longer needed!*

Had I been on a quiet country road and not on a thruway, I think I would have pulled off to the side and just sat staring into space. I wanted some time to absorb this stark judgment that my age had caused to be leveled against me. "Sorry, you're out. It's been nice knowing you, but you're no longer able to 'hack this job.' We need a younger man."

For the next few days I kept myself busy as I settled into the house where I was assigned for retirement. I had dozens of cartons of books and clothing to be unpacked, and I had my typewriter, radio and assorted gadgets to be uncrated and assembled. Concentration on these chores, I knew, would keep at bay that horrible sense of retirement's finality.

In the middle of a furious session of stuffing clothing in closets and books in bookcases, I took time out for a cup of coffee. I plopped myself at the big desk the room held and stared at the clutter of odds and ends my predecessor had left. I was about to sweep the mess into the wastebasket when my eye was caught by a small square of paper pasted against the base of the desk lamp. *"O, Lord,"* it read, *"keep me from living in the past; help me to press on with you to new ventures!"*

I found myself saying the words aloud — no, rather *praying* the words aloud. They were, after all, a prayer. I pushed back in the chair and closed my eyes and smiled. I could feel my fret over retirement's finality melt away. THIS TIME — THIS *NOW* — WAS REALLY A BEGINNING! As the popular saying expresses it: "Today is the first day of the rest of your life."

Whether you are retired or facing into retirement, I offer you what I think is one of the greatest little prayers we elders can say at this stage of our lives. As we face the challenge of our senior years, the words call for an awareness of our most important time — THE PRESENT!

God may have wrought a change in our life with retirement but if we believe in His will, it is because He has new work for us to do. This little prayer petitions for the grace to cooperate as He points out the new ventures we are to undertake and, in Him, accomplish. Try living this short prayer — I think you'll find you like it.

3   We Are Important

Of all the geriatric hazards I can think of, the most dangerous is falling prey to the feeling that we are not very important.

Recently, I sensed how pervasive this feeling can be. I was giving a triduum in honor of St. Ann at a residence for the elderly. In room after room that I visited during my stay at the residence, the occupant veered off from the general conversation we were having, to tell me that he or she didn't feel very much appreciated in life. They went on to comment that they "guessed that maybe that was to be expected. They were not very important to their family or anyone, anymore, anyway." The recurrent experiences moved me to drop a talk I'd scheduled and substitute an entirely different conference. This one had the title that I have used at the top of this brief meditation — "We *ARE* Important."

Too often, as we age, and family and friends die or move away, we get to feeling isolated, alone, out of things. We can become particularly sensitive to this mood if we are confined to a nursing home or elders' residence. Ultimately, this feeling degenerates into the depressing thought that we don't count for much in the busy world going on around us. We start to downgrade *our* lifetime accomplishments, *our* contributions to life, *our* ever having done anything that was very significant at all.

Let me review what I told my friends at the residence. St. Ann, I said, is a reminder that such thinking is absolute nonsense. Her name is found only in one apocryphal gospel and nowhere else. That one and rather chancy reference might make some claim that it shows how totally irrelevant and unimportant St. Ann was in history. She did nothing to warrant any mention of her in the authenticated New Testament story.

But how stupid these critics would show themselves to be! The one mention of St. Ann's name is as the mother of Mary from whom came the Savior of the world!

It is much the same with ourselves. We may not be mentioned at all in the history books of our world and time but we ARE IMPORTANT nonetheless. We are important in the ways we have given ourselves to God in the families we have raised or been members of. We are important in the care, time and attention we have shared with others. We are important in the thousands upon thousands of ways we have touched our world and tried to make it better.

We *are* important by the very fact that God used us as instruments ministering to the salvation of so many who have come into our lives. We *are* important as a Christian presence in the lives of others. Like St. Ann, we have shared ourselves that others might be saved — and THAT makes *US* very important.

4 Stay Front and Center

For the moment, let me remain on this theme of having a sense of being important. As with so many problems in our lives, feeling unimportant in our world can be traced to ourselves. We feel unimportant because we are beginning to think and act unimportant. We are letting ourselves be influenced too much by the stereotypical notions of what it means to be a senior citizen. We are accepting too many of the cliches about the elderly that fill our comic strips, the TV sit-coms, the movies.

Unthinkingly, almost entirely unaware, we let the cartoon image of the foxy grandpa and grandma take over. *THIS*, we get to telling ourselves, is how old folk act. We are old folk. This is how we should act. Old rockin' chair gets us because we are accepting of the stereotype that has been dunned at us since we were young ourselves.

Oh, of course, there is the gradual decline in the swiftness of our stride or the erectness of our posture. Yes, we may need glasses which persist in perching on the end of our nose or we have to settle for a denture or two as our own teeth quit being serviceable.

But, none of these renders us unimportant in life. We do that to ourselves by our attitude of heart and mind. It is our own outlook more often than not that makes us look, act and seem old. There is a ton of truth in the old saying that we are as old as we feel.

I can offer no better philosophy to guide us in our senior years than our title for this reflection: "Stay Front and Center." The world will attempt to shuffle us off to the background quick enough. It does this to young people as well as to the elderly. How many movie or TV stars, how many politicians, how many athletes — all young, vigorous, in the prime of life — has the world used up and cast aside after a season or two of attention and acclaim?

We must refuse to let it happen to us. We must remain as active as possible given the circumstances of our lives. Remember, God in His Holy Writ shows time and again, the needs and uses He has for the elderly. In the Old and New Testaments He calls them to demanding vocations, puts them to responsible efforts. It is only our culture which tries to ease the elderly off the scene and acts as if we belonged in that old rockin' chair.

With God, however, it is the opposite. The senior soul, the elderly man or woman is useful — and, as Scripture shows, USED by God — as long as he or she lives and to the extent that each wishes to cooperate with God in His plan for man.

Think of Elizabeth, Moses, Ann, Sarah, Nicodemus, Joseph of Arimathea, that long roster of senior citizens whom God called to work with Him in His plan of salvation for man.

He calls us as well.

Where we are and as we are, whatever our capacities, extensive or limited, God calls us to the same work.

Our obligation is to hear and heed the call, to stay

"Front and Center," fulfilling the job He gives us now in these our golden years.

5 You Are a Treasure, a Blessing

In our previous reflections, I stressed the fact that we seniors were important. As a matter of fact, very important to God. We see that God had often called upon the seniors of a community to carry out His special will and purpose. They were His chosen ones to get a job done.

Some might have smiled and thought that I was indulging in a bit of ego-building for seniors, trying to fluff up our spirits and make us all feel good about ourselves. Well, there is nothing wrong with making us all feel good, but it so happens that that was not what I was trying to do in my earlier reflections. I was serious about the fact that God in His Divine Providence has always seemed to depend heavily upon the elderly for the effecting of His will and work.

The Church Herself has followed this practice. Seniority stands for something in the Church. Our laws and practice and tradition are not gauged, as is so much in our modern society, to shuffle the elders into the background and get them out of the way. Experience has taught the Church through a long and arduous history that it takes time for a person to mature. She is not about to discard the fruits of that maturity because of the whims and impatience of the young to have a go at running things.

Positions of responsibility in the Church are not ordinarily dealt out to the kindergarten set you will notice. Gray hairs, seamed faces and wrinkled brows seem to be the more prevailing visage of our current crop of pastors, bishops, cardinals and the pope himself. Oh, yes, a junior member of the clergy may be appointed to some high ranking position but, ordinarily, this is unusual enough for it to be remarked upon.

For the Church, the elderly count and are important. Perhaps, the most trenchant words I've seen on this fact came from Pope John Paul II himself back in the early eighties when he was visiting Germany. He gave a talk on that visit to some seniors who were having an audience with him. He said to them in his introduction: "Brothers and Sisters of the older generation, you are a treasure for the Church, you are a blessing for the world."

The Pope continued much in this vein: "You are a necessary complement in a world which shows enthusiasm for the vitality of youth and for the power of the so-called 'best years.' You remind it that it continues building upon the diligence of those who have been young and strong earlier.

"In you it becomes apparent that the meaning of life cannot consist in earning and spending money, that in our external activities there has to mature something internal, and something eternal in all the temporal — according to the words of St. Paul: 'Though our outer nature is being wasted away, our inner nature is being renewed every day.'"

The Pope concluded his chat with the seniors by saying that he bows before old age and he invited all people to do the same with him. Old age, he said, is the crown of the steps of life. "Rich experience is the crown of the aged, and their boast is the fear of the Lord."

So, you see, this salute from Pope John Paul II only confirms what we have been saying. It is no idle statement to make when we say that seniors are important. They are, as Pope John Paul stated it to the seniors he addressed, "a treasure for the Church."

6 What's in a Name?

In a Harris survey a few years back, older adults were given a list of terms commonly used to describe their age group. They were asked to rate in the order of preference the name which they preferred when being referred to. "Mature Americans" was the top choice with 56% of the first-place votes.

The remainder of the list showed "Retired Persons" as second, chosen by 53%, and "Senior Citizens" was the third with 50%. Other terms on the selection list were "Middle-Aged Persons" and "Older Americans," both with 37%. "Golden-agers" was chosen by 27% of those voting and "Older Americans" had 27%. "Aged Persons" and "Old Men/Women" were the least popular terms. They managed only 19% and 9% of the vote respectively.

The list is an interesting insight into our sensitivity as to how we wish to be described as we add on those birthdays. I guess there is no harm in preferring a designation that is a little flattering and doesn't remind us too harshly of our gray hairs and wrinkles.

I offer the list, however, to make a special point for those of us who follow Christ.

The important thing for us — at any age, from cradle to grave — is not *WHAT* we are called but the fact *THAT* we are called. This special grace is something for which we should be grateful all our lives and particularly in these our later years. What a blessing to have been called by Christ into His friendship, to have a place near His Sacred Heart! What a bounty to have been brought to the shelter of His Church and the sharing of His sacraments! It makes worrying about *WHAT* we are called a vanity.

As we rest in the confidence of Christ's calling us, who

really cares about the titles given us at this stage of life? What's in a name after we have heard Christ say: "Come, all you who labor," or "Come apart with me and rest awhile"?

So, *WHAT* we are called matters little. *THAT* we have been called matters much — and *WHEN* we are called, it will matter most of all. Who really cares whether we are denoted as "Elder People" or "Golden Agers" or "Senior Citizens." The most important name we can be called will be the one we hear when Christ calls us "Thou good and faithful servant." That prelude to His invitation to enter into the kingdom prepared for us from all eternity is the most important designation we will ever hear.

7   But Not As Others See Us

I hate to disagree with one of my favorite quatrains in poetry but for our present reflection, I find I must.

The four lines from Robert Burns that I have quoted to myself innumerable times (and on which I have preached dozens of times) are:

> O wad some power the giftie gie us
> To see ourselves as others see us!
> It wad frae monie a blunder free us,
> An' foolish notion.

Burns' thought still has value and can well be taken to heart. At present, however, for seniors, the first two lines of the quatrain need some discussion. If there is one thing, we of the silver locks don't need to do — *shouldn't do* — is bother one whit with seeing ourselves as others see us.

We need to see ourselves as we are!

The image of the elderly portrayed so frequently in movies and on TV is NOT the stereotype we should permit to affect us and have us start imitating or fulfilling. Too many times, we are seen as backgrounders, fringe characters, people off whom the leading man or woman or leading funnyman or funnywoman can bounce a few smart lines of dialogue.

Admittedly, seniors are not given all that attention on prime time TV that we need raise a fuss about our image. Surveys show that though those over 60 make up about 15% of the population, prime time television devotes no more than 2% of its time dealing with them whether in documentaries or dramas or situation comedies. No matter; whether it's a little or a lot of attention we get, seniors are hardly ever front and center, the focus of the drama, the hub of the wheel around which others play at being spokes.

Fortunately for most of us, this is not a fact of our lives. We do not see ourselves as others see us, mere supernumeraries in the drama of life. At least, the people surveyed in Carol Kaufman's *The Ageless Self: Source of Meaning in Late Life* (University of Wisconsin Press) did not see themselves as backgrounders and props in the drama of their living. The book is a series of interviews with 60 seniors over the age of 70. The responses of the interviewees contradicted the popular view of old age as a distinct period of life. These people saw themselves as possessing a sense of continuity in an *ageless self* that exists amid changes across the span of their lives.

I think most of us would have tested as positively about who we are and who we see ourselves as being. How often we find in chatting with our contemporaries that someone will make the remark: "I just don't have any sense that I'm old." They are stating the basic fact that most of us recognize ourselves as a *person* not as a category called "The Old Aged."

If, by chance, we don't react this positively, it is time for self-examination and reaffirmation of our sense of individuality. God did not create us an old man or woman. God made us some *one* man or woman.

God loves us as *us* not as old-aged. God cherishes each of us as a person — someone who has experienced and who continues to experience life, not aging.

Thus, we should be about the Father's business of living life and not about the business of being totaled up merely as among the aged.

8   An Apostle, Anywhere, Anytime

I have been corresponding of late with a priest friend who is recovering from a very serious accident. He was struck by a car and suffered a fractured skull, a broken hip and pelvic bone, and crushed ribs on one side of his body.

Technically, he is retired but, until this accident, he had been one of the most active priests of his diocese. As you would suspect, it is the enforced inactivity, not the fractured skull and broken bones, that he is finding a burden these days.

He wrote about it recently and told me that, at first, he was in a frenzy to get back to work. He stated that he would wake in the morning and be fretful that he faced another day of being trussed up in bed, restricted in his movements with the height of his activity being no more than staring dumbly at a TV set opposite his bed.

Then, one day (his letter continued) one of the nurses walked into his room and thanked him for his help. He was puzzled by her gratitude since he couldn't recall having been of any assistance to her. She explained that at the time she had been assigned to his case she had been feeling very depressed and discouraged with her life. His cheerfulness, despite his calamity, had impressed her. It had made her realize that the inconveniences of her life were tiny compared to his major breaks and bruises. She admitted that he had made her see that she had little or nothing to be depressed over.

"She taught me," he wrote, "that I didn't have to be running about to be doing good. *Doing what I could, where I was*, and *under the circumstances I was in*, was still doing the Lord's work with, and for, His people."

These words are about the best reflection I could offer anyone at this time. What a slogan for our own advance in spirituality were we to write large over our days, *Do what we can, where we are, in the life-situation to which God has assigned us.*

As seniors, curtailment of activities, containment in getting about, restrictions of time and place and circumstances are so much a part of our lives. They do tend to make us chafe at our limitations. We recollect our younger days, the freedom, the facility with which we got about, the calls we could respond to, all the great plans we ambitioned doing for the Lord. The memories stir us to the edge of grumbling about the state God has placed us in now, in our limiting and advancing years. We are ready to take our complaints to Mary and our favorite saints and have them side with us as we plan to give God "come what."

Don't bother. Recollect my saintly priest friend on that bed in the hospital with half his body broken and busted. He learned that where he is and in the condition he is in, he is doing what God needs to get done now.

God is asking cooperation from him, not complaints.

Wherever we are, however we are, remember the message: God is asking cooperators, not complainers. The latter do not get His work done. The former do.

9 With God First, All Things are in Order

I wonder if some of our popular writers and commentators who lament the world's evil and moan over its staggering crime rate ever realize that no evil or crime on which they comment is an isolated manifestation of human failure. The murder, the rape, the arson, the robbery, the breech of contract, this violation of law or that, is merely part of a whole picture, part of a totality of sin that all goes together.

The disorder in the world comes from the fundamental disorder fostered by the modern attitude which tells man that he comes first. As to God? Well, let God fit in afterwards as best He can.

This attitude now puts US in charge and with US in the driver's seat, the direction you see the world taking is the direction it will continue to pursue until someone restores reason and order to the hierarchy of values we are living by. As the saying goes, what you see is what you get.

With US in charge, there are only our rules and laws, which we make for ourselves and which we can keep or break or change as we please. If we find a law inconvenient, harsh, difficult, we can cry: "Get rid of it!" Our demand is that society make us a more pleasant law, a more lenient one. After all, we say, you only live once and you have the right to be pleasured and free and able to do your thing. Ultimately, in this kind of world, we all end up playing at being God.

What is the remedy?

It is to be found in the very first commandment. I AM THE LORD THY GOD, THOU SHALT NOT HAVE STRANGE GODS BEFORE ME. We must practice — and, in turn, teach our world — this important lesson: Get God FIRST and things will be in their good, right, correct and proper order. In the proper order, the world will find itself a safer and happier place.

As seniors we know that it can take a lifetime to learn this lesson. But, our lifetime will be worthwhile only if we learn the lesson and live it.

We might offer the learning and the living of this lesson as a prayer for our world. Pray that it learn to reshape its priorities soon — before it is too late.

10 In God — We Live Ever Young

> I have an enormous, almost religious faith in the biological resilience, the ability of the human body and mind to keep fit and continue developing. I always tell my medical students to remember that their patients . . . have enormous reserves . . . the human body and mind have enormous powers of recuperation.
>
> (Dr. Rene J. Dubos)

I would be among the first who would subscribe to those remarks I have quoted at the beginning of our reflection. They come from an interview given by Dr. Rene Dubos, an expert in the field of geriatrics.

I have believed all my life that we do not live up to our potential at any time in our lives. It's not a very original thought. There are countless studies that confirm what I've written.

One of the sad notes about the excellent interview with Dr. Dubos was that throughout the whole discussion he had on age and aging, he remained almost totally on the natural level. With all his experience, the good doctor never got to the supernatural aspects of our lives as he encouraged older people to learn, and to live to, the depth of reserves we possess.

Would that this learned octogenarian had given the tiniest nod to the spiritual reserves upon which we may draw to increase what he describes as "biological resilience." Too bad Dr. Dubos didn't recall the words of the psalmist as he sang: "Bless the Lord, my soul . . . thy youth shall be renewed like the eagles."

Our reserves might be biological in part but in the complete picture they are spiritual as well. As Christians we know that we never feel "peppier" or sounder or more ambitious than when we have joined ourselves to God in fervent prayer. We know we are "up" for any task when we have received Him in His sacraments or celebrated with Him in His Mass.

The will and the drive — no matter what years we count — to do things, to push on to the new, to undertake extra ventures is greatest when we live in, and through, and by, God's renewing help.

Natural resilience can take us just so far. If we really want to accomplish, to achieve in these senior years, we best do it with our "youth" renewed like the eagles — by God, in God, for God.

11   The Bottom Line

One of the current popular expressions that we hear repeated under so many circumstances of life is "What's the bottom line?" or "Get to the bottom line."

The expression obviously comes from the world of business and the matter of business reporting. If you are at all familiar with the annual reports that large corporations send out, you know that they are filled with pages and pages of material that the average stockholder never bothers to look at. The stockholder is interested in only one line that is down at the end of all the financial graphs and columns on assets and liabilities. He's interested in the last line of this array of figures. Does it show a profit or a loss?

Simply, he wants to know beyond all the explanations, excuses, predictions and qualifying statements of the corporation chairman: What does the bottom line show? Did the company make or not make some money for its stockholders?

As appropriated by our society, the expression has become a very telling and incisive one for cutting through verbiage. When people are trying to get the facts or the truth of a report or review of some situation, a medical or business report, for instance, they don't want to be given too much fluff and filling. They do not want cover-up, they want to see the final verdict or conclusion on the situation under consideration. They want to see the bottom line.

Speaking of appropriating, we seniors might well do a little appropriating of the phrase ourselves for making a judgment on our spiritual condition. As we review our lives and make a report to ourselves, is there any better question to ask than: What's the bottom line? Does it show a profit or a loss? Does it show we are people well aware of the really important place that prayer, devotion and a sense of the presence of God should have in our lives?

If it doesn't, then our bottom line is due for some changing by the time the next report on the state of our spiritual life is due. God is good in giving us time to review our lives and right the minuses that might be showing on our report. We should thank Him for the life He gives us yet to turn any possible minus into a plus. And, it behooves us to do just that.

More significantly, if we come to our senior years almost estranged from God and the spiritual values He represents, we know that our bottom line is reading minus. We know that it is time to do some balancing out of the importance of the earthly against the eternal. Having seen so much of life pass by, having seen the right come and go, the famous enjoy their brief day in the sun, the wielders of power gain a few headlines for no more than a moment, we are qualified to make a most serious judgment on the lastingness and importance of money, fame or power. We would have to be addle-brained not to repeat with Christ, "What does it profit a man to gain the whole world, and suffer the loss of his immortal soul?"

We well know that money, fame and power have availed nothing by way of escaping death or judgment for the rich or the famous or the powerful who have died and passed into eternity. Realistically, we can conclude, little of the world's goods or glories will avail us. As have all the rich, famous or powerful judged before us, we will face a review of the bottom line on our lives. Does it show that we have loved God with our whole heart, our whole mind and our whole soul?

Now is the time to ready our answer to God's question at the moment of judgment: What does the bottom line say? Now, as St. Paul says, is the acceptable time. *Now* is the time to make certain that our bottom line is a plus.

After *now*, it will be too late.

SECTION TWO

The Past

But I've left the Past in God's keeping
— the Future His mercy shall clear.

Mary Gardiner Brainard

12 Forget the Past

A recent hospital call on an old parishioner has decided me to continue, for the moment, in this vein of recommending that we push away from the past and look forward. Particularly do I make this a recommendation in the matter of past sins.

My dear hospitalized friend wanted to do exactly the opposite. I spent the best part of my visit dissuading her from her desire to go over all her past life which in its early years had been a crazy, mixed-up sort of thing. Happily, I succeeded in preventing her from trailing out all the frets and fears she was suffering over past sins.

This morbid tendency to pick over past sins and worry about them — and whether or not they have been forgiven — seems to be like graying hairs and wrinkles for many of the elderly. It's part of the package that comes with the onset of old age. Unlike graying hairs and wrinkles, however, it is not just something that happens and can be gracefully accepted. For those afflicted, it is a torturous situation, often destructive of peace of mind and soul to the point of making them ill.

For these souls — for all of us seniors — God gives the best counsel I know. In Isaiah 43:18-19 we can read these encouraging words:

Remember not the events of the past,
The things of long ago consider not;
See, I am doing something new . . .
Do you not perceive it?

This is God telling us that what is past is past and there is
nothing to be gained by living it over and over again —
especially those parts of the past which might have been
sinful, less worthy of us as Christians. In our lives of striving
to be united with Him now, He is working on "doing something new" in and with us. As St. Paul writes, we have been
reborn, we have put on the "newness" of Christ.

Those who find in themselves a tendency to this morbid
rehashing of the past, especially past offenses against God,
should be of good heart. There need be no dread of judgment and God's going over of the past. He won't be going
over it all, at all. He'll be going over the good you do and
have done, not the evil you might have done.

So — lift up your hearts — get on to the doing of good.
Leave those yesterdays right back where they are. That past
is for forgetting, not regretting. Remember — God says so!
What He does with you now — and what you do with Him —
is something new.

13   Good and Bad Memories

Our most casual dipping into newspapers and magazines
dedicated to seniors shows that we, as a group, are studied,
polled, canvased and checked out to a fare-thee-well. What
we eat and drink, what we think, where we live, what we

wear, how we vote, what our favorite TV shows are, are charted in survey after survey. Our brains, attitudes, responses, likes and dislikes are measured and mapped to give the curious and the concerned a profile on what makes us tick.

Some years back, the magazine *Changing Times* had an interesting study about the shifts that take place in seniors as they age. The part of the article that remained with me most forcefully was the section devoted to the mystery of memory in the elderly. The author especially focused on the tendency for our memory to fade as we age.

He described two kinds of memory, "primary" and "secondary." Without going into an involved discussion on these kinds of memory, I can sum up the point he was making.

As we age, we are less likely to retain "new" information. Because of a number of factors, it falls into the category of "secondary." We may judge this information to be unnecessary, unimportant, not useful for us to survive. We tend to let go of it quickly and easily. That memory which is important and necessary — "primary" — we tend to make every effort to retain and do retain it almost as well as any other age group in our society.

For our reflection here, I'd like to borrow those categories, "primary" and "secondary." I'd like to apply them to define certain memories we all carry with us. I would call "primary," those memories we have of the good things that have happened in our lives. Among these, of course, would be those memories of the good people and the good things they have done for us.

I call "secondary," the unhappy things that have happened to us, especially the injustices, slights, hurts, the pains and heartbreak that others have caused us. These could range from some minor uncharitableness to a vicious personal attack that wounds us deeply enough to leave a lasting scar.

In my distinction of "primary" and "secondary," our striving should be to practice a quick and easy forgetfulness of these "secondary" memories. This is a forgetfulness that we might better cultivate than to sit and let fester the afflictions we might have suffered from others.

We are old enough to have learned that there is little profit to holding grudges, remembering insults, going over some injustice. There is nothing more destructive to enjoying our senior years than letting the "bad parts" of the past rule our hearts and souls. Having been hurt once, why permit these things to hurt now when peace of mind and soul is so much to be cherished?

We should spend these senior years in a joyful remembrance of the good things and good times that God has given us — and we all know they are many.

Besides, forgiving and forgetting is being more like Christ. And, as Christians, being like Christ is what we profess ourselves to become.

14   A Past To Live By

One of the highest compliments you can pay some people today is to describe them as "very progressive." So many love to think that they are on the cutting edge of our culture that they will go to extremes in their words and actions to prove that they are in the "frontest" ranks of our society's Front Rankers. The competition to be first with the new, or first to breach an old barrier, or first to violate an ancient tradition is truly fierce. There are occasions when it seems to be tinged with madness.

Granted, not all progressiveness is wrong or harmful. Not all advanced thinking, new ideas or inventions are to be condemned and shunned. Who would want to give up the electric bulb for an oil lamp or tallow candle? Who would be fool enough to petition that we junk jet airplane traveling and return to the hazards and hardships of the old stagecoach or the three-masted schooner?

Progressiveness for its own sake, however, can be manic. Just as well, it can be foolish and capricious when it is advanced out of self-servicing, whim, boredom or unreasonable discontent with what is old and what is past. In fact, progress that springs from these motives is more accurately immaturity and selfishness masquerading as progressiveness.

More important, if the rage for the new, the strange, the exotic, the different could endanger a soul, a halt must be called to it. When progressiveness leads a soul from true values, or, tragically, it attempts to destroy those values, it must be challenged.

The Church is the wonderful gift of God to us that enables us to review constantly our own perspective on our approach to the swirl of progressiveness infecting our world today. The Church holds a past that is rooted in Christ. It is an enduring past, a tested past, a past by which we may live certain. It is *THE PAST* by which we may live.

We are able with and through the Church to examine our perspective on Christ's message given to Peter and the other apostles. Jesus' instruction to His chosen twelve was "Teach whatsoever I have commanded you" (Mt 28:20). Our security is in Him and in His promise that the Holy Spirit, the Spirit of Truth would be with these men on whom He built His Church.

We can test anything progressive that is offered us today by our ecclesiastical pundits, our popular theologians and/or theorists. No matter what the field in which these people roam and make their pronouncements — morals, dogma, Scripture, liturgy, sacraments, devotions, you name it — their statements can be put to an immediate judgment. Is that what the Church teaches?

That is our guarantee of security on the means by which God makes it possible for us to be saved. Christ's words, "He who hears you, hears me" (Lk 10:16), resound down, as Francis Thompson describes it, "the arches of the years."

We need not be fretted or harried by all the waves of newness swirling about the Church today. That solidly built Barque of Peter has ridden out — believe it — worse storms than today's onslaught of secularism and modernism.

All we need remember is that the Church of Christ is the tester, the definer, the judge of all that is new and progressive. Possess your soul in peace. Christ promised, "I will not leave you orphans" (Jn 14:18). And He has not. He has given us the Church which is mother, father, sister and brother for us.

It is guardian, guide and guarantor of all proper progressiveness — at least, all the progressiveness we will ever need to achieve heaven.

SECTION THREE

Prayer

And it came to pass, that as He was
in a certain place praying, when He ceased,
one of His disciples said to Him: "Lord,
teach us to pray . . ."

Luke 11:1

15   Find Time For Prayer

Recently I was preparing a talk for some older retreatants and one of our novices asked me what I planned to speak on.

I replied, "I'm going to tell them to be sure always to find time for prayer."

My reply came as a surprise to the young man. "Do older people need to be told that?" he asked, and continued, "I'd think that was something they had plenty of time for and seldom missed doing."

God bless his innocence, I thought. It was obvious that he had a lot to learn about humanity, and about seniors. Advancing years do not usher us into some phase of life where we automatically find — or make — great gobs of time for God. Many seniors do no more praying in their sixties and their seventies that they did in their teens.

Finding time to pray is a matter of practice. It is a habit. It must be repeated and cultivated all the days of our lives.

Chat sometime with priests and religious and ask them about this matter of prayer life. If they are truly frank they will admit that one of the easiest bad habits to fall into is letting their prayer life slip and slide away. They can tell you how many times the slightest reason can be used to skip prayer. Of course, there are legitimate ruptures to a prayer schedule. Most of us understand these and their existence does not bother us. What nags our conscience is allowing the minor interruptions — the unnecessary chore, the unimportant telephone conversation, the delay over a book or with a casual visitor — to become major interruptions in our routine of prayer.

The worst aspect of these self-indulgences is that when we permit too many of these excuses to take us from prayer, we soon find that we have a fight with our fallen nature on our hands. We actually have to struggle with ourselves to resume our old prayerful ways.

Wisdom dictates that we be realistic about the efforts we'll be forced to put forth all our lives to keep faithful to the habit of prayer. We must resist always the temptations that suggest we skip our prayers or shorten them or perform them at a later time. Need I repeat here what I wrote above? Of course, there are legitimate reasons for interrupting a prayer routine. God forbid we turn ourselves into rigid martinets who hold to a schedule while the world around us is in dire crisis and crying for help. (Our good judgment, I'm sure, can be trusted to make the distinction between the important and the unimportant interruption to prayer.)

Above and beyond all this, however, whether there are interruptions or not, whatever the vicissitudes of life that militate against a sound routine of prayers, the one and necessary thing is — ALWAYS FIND SOME TIME FOR PRAYER!

Remember that old saying: "The person who is too busy to pray is just too busy."

No one can be *too busy* to talk with God sometime through each day that He generously gives us.

16   Any Age is a Good Age for Spirituality

I suppose someone could mount a challenge to me and ask what I mean by discussing spirituality for seniors. After all, the challenge might go, isn't spirituality just spirituality? Isn't it attempting and striving for closer union with God, a deepening of one's sense of His presence and power in our lives? Isn't that sense of the spiritual something we all pursue irrespective of any particular age bracket we happen to be in? Does a First Communicant at seven have less obligation toward striving for perfection than an octogenarian receiving the sacrament of the sick?

Not being the argumentative type, I would have to admit that the search for sanctity is not something that can be partitioned off. It is the job we are all on for all of our lives. The obligation is full, whole, total no matter what birthday we are celebrating. No age provides a period in which we can take it easy on this job.

Despite all this, I think there is some validity to specializing or particularizing this "following of Christ." It may be entirely arbitrary but I see no reason why we cannot concentrate our efforts on spiritualizing seniors.

True, our sense of purpose of life, our intention to know, love and serve God need to be firm and fixed all through our lives. Yet, the things we can do, the works we can perform, the way we are able or capable of "following" may shift drastically for the elderly as contrasted with what they were capable of in their teens or the prime of life.

When you are laid up with lumbago or crippled by severe arthritis, you are not able, nor are you about to attempt, to spiritualize life on the same scale as the persons fifty years younger. When we are twenty, for example, our prayer is aspirational, forward looking, tending toward attaining natural and supernatural goals. Shift that prayer activity to someone who is seventy and you find that the prayer becomes more reflective, inclines toward the making of frequent reviews on the life lived. We tend in prayer to start measuring how well the goals set were met throughout life.

Looked at this way, it becomes obvious that there is nothing wrong with stressing spirituality for one age group — seniors. Quite possibly, it is more important for seniors than for other age groups who would normally get attention. As we wrote early in these pieces, seniors tend to get overlooked. They are given credit for having been through it all, having seen it all, and not needing any help in coping with life.

As we've learned, this is so far from the truth it isn't worth debating. If there was ever a time when we needed the comfort of spiritual guidance, old age is that time. There may not be too much such counsel around but I recommend that you avail yourselves of all that is offered.

17   The Poor Souls

Our thoughts as we reflect on the Poor Souls will necessarily be directed outward rather than inward for a change. I'm sure we agree that it can't impede our spirituality to think, for the moment, of others. It is, after all, a most Christian way of living. In fact, it is the way Christians are supposed to live always. Where Plato said, "Conquer yourself," and Aristotle said, "Know yourself," Christ came along and preached, "Give yourself."

I must admit that I never tire of devotion to the Poor

Souls. Having learned the devotion well from a dear old Irish grandmother, it has remained a favorite spiritual practice of mine through a lifetime. As well, I never missed an opportunity to preach on the devotion in the years I gave parish missions.

There is an unfortunate tendency growing among us Catholic priests these days to "canonize" just about anyone we bury. I suppose there is nothing terribly wrong with assigning a place in heaven to a departed parent or relative, to a good friend or to a solidly pious parishioner. Certainly, we WANT them to be with God and His Blessed Mother. And just as certainly, we know that THEY WANTED to achieve heaven as they persevered in their efforts to live up to the demands of our Faith.

The danger in this kind of "immediate canonization" is that we might tend to neglect praying for our dear departed souls on the assumption that since they rest joyfully in heaven, they have no great want of our prayers. I don't wish to be a spoilsport but I feel we'd be better off assuming that these dear souls who go before us NEED our prayers.

I don't say that you have to put credence in the somewhat sobering revelations of some mystics about purgatory and the souls who delay there; nor do I suggest that you must concentrate on the revelations concerning purgatory made by the Blessed Mother to the children who are reported to have talked with her at Fatima. Just take my word for it — I think that we and the Poor Souls will be better off if we pray for them and make no assumptions about their being in heaven. If they are enjoying the glory of the Beatific Vision, we know our prayers are not wasted. God will dispose of our charitable efforts justly for the souls who might need the extra prayers. If, on the other hand, our dear departed still delay in purgatory, our prayers will serve them well in their need.

I guess my devotion to the Poor Souls is a bit of playing it safe. I don't delude myself into thinking that I'll make heaven in one quick jump from my last breath to my entering into eternity. I must admit, I hope to make purgatory. That means I'll need prayers myself. I am gambling that if, in my lifetime, I manage to move a few souls heavenward by my prayers and sacrifices, they'll be exhorting God to grant me swift passage to heaven. It's what I call my spiritual insurance business.

What I am really doing is urging you to live the fact and reality of the Communion of Saints. Prayers for the faithful departed are a demonstration of the Church Militant helping the Church Suffering to become the Church Triumphant. I recommend the practice highly. It can't hurt the Poor Souls in purgatory — or, eventually, for that matter — *YOU*.

18   Remembrances of Nana

Our previous reflection on the Poor Souls and the Communion of Saints has caused a flood of memories to rise in me. I am brought back to my childhood and days of growing up around my paternal grandmother. I haven't the slightest doubt in the world that many of the devotional attitudes and practices I've acquired in life are from association with my old Irish Nana. They are very simple, basic pieties that involve the Blessed Mother, the Sacred Heart, statues, the rosary, guardian angels, vigil candles and the like. I make no apologies for them since they have stood me in good stead all my life.

I count myself as most fortunate that I lived in the same

house as she, in the years I was attending grade school. I had inherited from a young aunt the job of having to take Nana to morning Mass at our parish church. As you would suspect, she attended the first and earliest Mass. I had to be up around 5:30 each morning and make sure Nana was at church by 6:15 A.M. for her preparation for Mass and Communion.

Most every evening after dinner, a visit with Nana was a must. There was no fooling around in those visits. Those sessions usually meant the reciting of the rosary with a long string of prayers that followed it. These prayers covered all Nana's intentions and these seemed to cover all the counties of Ireland where she had relatives and friends.

The month of November was the time I remember most vividly. Then, the prayers after the rosary got longer. As Nana explained it, we were putting all our efforts into moving the family's Poor Souls out of purgatory into heaven. There were evenings when I would wonder drowsily if she intended that not just our family souls but *all* the souls in purgatory must be moved heavenward.

I smile now as I recollect those days and Nana shaking me to keep me awake. I don't smile at the recollection of the devotion for the Poor Souls that she instilled in me. I must admit that every November, my own prayers take on that long string of intentions as I pray to do a little "moving job" of my own on behalf of the Faithful Departed.

I must admit that many, many years ago, as a sleepy youngster kneeling and telling the beads with my grandmother in her living room, I thought all this moving of souls to heaven was an admirable and exemplary, but private whim of hers. A little Scripture study in the seminary taught me better. This idea of moving souls along comes right our of Sacred Writ.

You may recall the story. In the Second Book of Maccabees (12:43-46), we find that Judas Maccabeus has collected silver to be offered at the temple in Jerusalem for his soldiers who had fallen in battle. His reason for the offering and the prayers was as simple — and, I'm sure, as efficacious — as that of my grandmother. He told those interested that "it is a holy and a wholesome thought to pray for the dead. . . ."

Yes, we have reflected on the Poor Souls in a previous consideration. Somehow, I think such reflection bears repeating. Since we teach that under their present circumstances the Faithful Departed are unable to help move themselves to heaven, why not learn, as I did, a lesson from Nana? Why not take over their cause with our prayers and, in praying and sacrificing, bring them to union with Christ and His Blessed Mother, Mary?

I can think of no other memorial we might give for the dead that surpasses our prayers for them.

19 The Eucharist: Remedy for What Ails Us

Throughout all ages man has dreamed of and hoped for a panacea. He has searched for a cure-all, some medicine, even the quackiest, that would heal the ailments and afflictions that have plagued the human race since Adam and Eve bade farewell to the delights of the Garden of Eden.

As history attests, up to this date, no such panacea has been discovered or manufactured. Generation after generation of us still contend with the minor croups and catarrhs, breaks and lesions that hamper and hinder us through life. Too, we face as bravely as we can into the major ills to which we succumb ultimately and die.

In our time, more so it seems than at any other age, the search for a panacea for the ills of the mind outranks our search for a cure-all for sicknesses of the body. Pills by the tonful literally pour out of our pharmaceutical plants, bottles and bags and boxes of hope for humankind afflicted by depression, psychosis, hysteria, hyperactivity, manic-depression and all the other complaints raised today by those mentally and psychologically disturbed.

As with the problems that afflict the body, no panacea has been found to treat and eliminate from the human race, the problems of the mind. It seems that generation after generation confronts the same afflictions of the one preceding it. Devastating tensions, breakdowns, spiritual crack-ups appear anew and the pharmaceutical factories go to work on new pills and potions and powders.

All the while a divine panacea exists, waiting for man to turn to it, take it, use it, be healed by it. The panacea is the Holy Eucharist, instituted by Christ. His institution of this sacrament was for the purpose of giving us peace of heart and mind, and strength and power to accept and live with the weakness of our bodies.

Page through the gospel story and follow the incidents where Christ promised and, then, fulfilled His promise of the Eucharist. Here we have definite, striking truth that the Eucharist is THE cure-all man has been seeking for his hurts of body and mind.

Space does not permit running through all the texts that are significant but consider these: "He who eats my flesh and drinks my blood has life everlasting and I will raise him up on the last day"; "If you do not eat the flesh of the Son of Man, and drink His blood, you do not have life in you" (Jn 6:54, 53).

No, Christ isn't promising to heal ulcers or cure cancer or eliminate AIDS. This panacea of the Eucharist is the ultimate healer, the cure-all for the worst of physical afflictions we can suffer — death. *That* actually is what all the search for a panacea has been about. When brought to its logical conclusion the quest of the human race to heal its ills shows that quest to be for immortality. Man fights to cure these little deaths of broken bones and bruised limbs and degenerated organs. We recognize all these little deaths as signs of our impermanency as creatures. Could we but conquer them, we tell ourselves, and we are well on the way to conquering death itself.

As regards the mind and its weaknesses, warps and wounds, nothing equals the Eucharist as panacea. With proper spiritual guidance and, of course, some professional counseling, it can bring comfort and hope and solace for the depressed. As well, for the nervous, it will bring quiet and calm and serenity. Christ promised — and will not fail in promising "Come to me, all you who labor and are burdened, and I will refresh you" (Mt 11:28).

Our intense devotion to the Eucharist should be put to teaching the world that the panacea so avidly and earnestly sought is here. Unlike the pie-in-the-sky methods man has employed, the Blessed Sacrament works on body and soul. Again, we don't expect it to work miracles with a broken leg or faltering heart. We do expect it to settle us and our fears in handling bodily ailments.

It is tragic that in recent decades, devotion to the Blessed Sacrament has been allowed to decline. The traditional Eucharistic practices of years back — making the Forty Hours or a Eucharistic Day of Retreat or a Holy Hour or even brief, simple visits to the Blessed Sacrament — have about disappeared from the devotional life of the Catholic Church. I would guess that the loneliest place in many towns these days is right before the tabernacle of the local parish church.

In whatever way we can intensify our attitude of devotion to the Eucharist we should put it to use in rekindling and renewing that former beautiful, inspiring love of the Eucharist for which the Church was renowned.

The world wants a panacea. Give it the one God gave it and which it seems to know so little about — the Blessed Sacrament. Give it Christ, really living, entire, waiting, in His Eucharistic presence.

That Presence is panacea.

20   Sword of Deliverance

I don't think I surprise you by saying that the Church has problems today. Big problems. All is not sweetness and light with us as some would like to believe or would like us to believe. In fact, if we ran off a list of all the problems, we might find ourselves a-tremble at viewing the state we are in.

If we can believe the polls taken (and so very apparently announced with a kind of spiteful glee by the secularist-controlled media [radio, TV and newspapers]), we Catholics show absolutely no difference in our moral mentality from the worldliest of the worldly. The polls say that great and grievous percentages of us believe in divorce, birth prevention, abortion (in some instances), homosexuality, premarital sex, and so on and on and on ad nauseam. You name the world's shabbiest attitude on any moral tenet and Catholics are quoted and demonstrated as matching the percentages of people with little or no religious affiliation. And these percentages advanced for us are in direct contradiction to the *official* teaching of the Church since the time of Christ and the apostles.

Worse, for us, is the fact that our catechetics and the teaching of it are a shambles. We have a generation of young Catholics coming along who have been described in knowledgeable quarters as "catechetically, religiously and devotionally illiterate." They are alleged to have weighed the Church and found it wanting.

Perhaps, the greatest indicator of the state we are in is the one talked of as the "vocation crisis." Churches are being shuttered, parishes merged, and schools closed or combined because the young men and women on whom we depend as the resource to keep these fundamental factors operating have refused en masse to consider serving God and the Church. Dedicating their lives to the communicating and preserving of the Faith is the furthest thing from their minds.

I wouldn't dare hazard a plan for turning this situation around. Thank God, our capable and courageous John Paul II is at work on this project now. Yet, it is obvious he is having a mighty struggle to be effective in a refusing and resenting age of tepid and worldly Catholics.

I would, however, offer a way to cooperate with Pope John Paul. Do what you can to restore devotion to Mary in the Church. Love and devotion to Mary has, as have so many other things we held traditionally sacred, come on hard times. It *must* be reasserted if we are to renew all things in Christ.

Mary was committed to us by Christ from the cross. In turn, we, through St. John, were committed to her. Church history has proved that without her we are orphans. It has proved, as well, that when Mary is preached, venerated and loved, the Church shines forth to the world as One, Holy, Catholic and Apostolic. The great ages of faith have been Marian Ages where through fierce and zealous devotion to her the world was brought to Christ.

Her great prayer is the Rosary. It has been called her Sword of Deliverance. Pray it these days as you have never prayed it before and if you have never prayed it before, start doing it now. Pray it for Mary's return soon to prominence in Catholic devotions, sermons, families, lives. Put this powerful Sword of Deliverance behind Pope John Paul II and his efforts to restore all things in Christ.

I know no other way by which renewal of the Church can be accomplished. It will be through Mary or, tragically, not at all. Use the Rosary, Mary's Sword of Deliverance, so that true renewal for a troubled Church can be accomplished.

21 Do What You Can — I

You are probably on as many charitable institutions' mailing lists as I am. No day goes by without one, two or three of these appeals filling out my mail box at the seminary. I read them all compulsively. I just don't have the heart not to pay some attention to an appeal even if I know as I slit open the envelope that I am not going to be able to respond to it. I feel the apostolate asking my help deserves the benefit and the courtesy of a hearing.

It breaks my heart not to be able to give something to every appeal. I squirm uncomfortably when I read the folders from these mission societies of priests, brothers or sisters and recognize the abysmal conditions under which they labor. If the folder carries photographs of the people to whom they minister and shows the despairing conditions of their charges, I am miserable tearing up the appeal and discarding the request for help in a critical and deplorable situation.

Yet, we cannot respond to every plea that is made to us. Sadly, we have to pick out those that are something of a favorite or answer those from the community in which we have a friend or relative who has first call on whatever financial response we can make.

There is something we can do and that is pray for each and every one of the appeals we receive. Here is a response we all can make to these urgent and heartrending solicitations for funds we get in the mail. It may not prove much solace to the "mailers" of these appeals staring at their bills and learning that you are going to pray for their cause. If, however, they are people of faith, it should excite them. As men and women of faith, they should know you are putting behind their apostolate one of the most powerful weapons that can be found. They should recall Tennyson's telling counsel that "More things are wrought by prayer than this world dreams of."

Realistically, we know we cannot answer all the begging letters we receive from the missions. But, praying for each appeal you receive is a matter of doing what you can. One nice thing about this is that while there is a limit to the riches of your pocketbook, there is no limit to the largess you can dispense with prayer. All of your life can be used for this intention, praying for all the missions that send out appeals to us.

In this way we can cooperate, can be a part of every appeal that stirs us and leaves us yearning to help.

We can become missionaries and supply prayer, the key that will open heaven's treasures for the mission fields and the laborers in the vineyard.

22 Do What You Can — II

In our previous reflection, I exhorted seniors to pray for the missions and missionaries in lieu of being able to respond financially to all mission appeals made to us.

I would like to remain in that vein of thought as we contemplate another situation that has become so critical for the Catholic Church — particularly in North America and Europe — in this age. It is the matter of vocations in general, but vocations to the priesthood in particular.

Among the appeals we receive, many are from seminaries asking for financial support for the vocations the particular diocese or the religious community has in training. Many make the special plea for us to create a burse in memory of our parents or for some special intention we cherish.

As with all such appeals, our spirits are willing but our pocketbooks are anemic. Why couldn't it be a special senior apostolate to take some seminarian and support him by prayers and sacrifices until he is ordained!

Seminary life is not easy for the young men who embrace it today. It never was easy but in our age, temptations seem more enticing, stability seems less developed in some of the men, and defections from the seminary are appalling. Statistics reveal that seminary enrollment has dropped almost 65 to 75%! Obviously that means that in the years ahead, the Church in North America and Europe will have that percentage fewer priests to serve it. Even now, in many sections of the United States, the crisis has grown to proportions where parishes have had to be closed or merged for lack of men to serve them.

We agreed previously that many seniors just cannot afford to commit themselves to the fairly substantial financial contributions a seminary burse program demands. The question arises — in that case is all lost? Is there no chance for us to participate in the "making" of a priest in a very personal manner?

I don't think so. Why is it not possible for any of us to make a real powerhouse contribution by donating our daily prayers, Masses, Holy Communions, Rosaries, Stations of the Cross and the like to some particular seminarian? And, what about that most choice of an elder's gifts that can be given — the aches and pains, the loneliness and depression, the burdens and inconveniences of advancing old age? What a storehouse of gifts is here for some young man struggling to achieve his dream of advancing to God's altar to offer the Holy Sacrifice of the Mass and minister to His people!

The choice does not have to be someone by name. If that can be arranged by writing to some seminary or contacting some priest friend who would choose someone for you, all well and good. All that is necessary, however, would be for us to make an intention and ask the Blessed Mother to apply all the spiritual gifts I delineated above to that seminarian most in need of assistance.

This is a real and practical suggestion. I know, because I have friends who are now praying and working for seminarians whom I have assigned to them.

There may be a vocation shortage in candidates applying to the priesthood. We can and should be offering prayers for the easing of this, too. There need be *no shortage* in this vocation of praying for the perseverance of those men already studying for the sacrament of Holy Orders.

All of us seniors can fulfill this call. In our own personal, special way, we should fulfill it and work to give God priests for His altar and for His people.

23 Distractions in Prayer

In this poll-taking world in which we live, where we are asked our attitudes on everything from what breakfast food we eat to what we think of nuclear fission vs. nuclear fusion, there is one question I am POSITIVE need not be polled. The question is: "What is the greatest problem you have with your prayer?"

I know that *distractions* is the answer most people will give should they be polled on that question. It is the bane of all our lives as we make efforts to unite ourselves to God in prayer.

Sadly, it becomes for some a veritable source of serious anxiety. They feel that their prayers are a total waste. They dread approaching prayer because they see themselves as displeasing God with further fractured efforts to talk to Him.

Be of good heart! All we need do is glance at a crucifix and recollect the three hours of Christ on Calvary and we recognize an example of a distracted prayer that should prove an enduring consolation to us. In the greatest prayer that was ever prayed — Christ's dying on the cross — we see Him distracted from start to finish. Our dear Lord was never allowed to concentrate on His divine prayer for our salvation.

If it was not the pain He suffered distracting Him, it was the mob shouting at Him, or the Good Thief asking for mercy, or Christ's own concern for His Blessed Mother.

Take heart! Obviously, Our Lord knows all about distraction in prayer. The hours on Calvary were crowded with them, yet Christ prayed the most effective prayer the world is to know.

The distractions of your prayer time will not be as many

or as monumental as were Christ's. True, they will plague your prayer as Christ's distractions plagued Him.

Just do what He did under all distractions. He persevered in His prayer.

Pain/Suffering

There are gains for all our losses,
There are balms for all our pains.

The Flight of Youth
Richard Henry Stoddard

24 Affliction

The dictionary defines *affliction* as a condition and/or cause of pain, suffering or distress.

Affliction is something all of us would readily do without, if we had our druthers. We are all subject to it throughout all of our lives. The first bump on the head we suffer as an infant is initiation and welcome to the gang. That first lump on our baby skull confers upon us a lifetime membership in the club of hurting humanity.

As we get older, affliction seems to become the pervasive condition of our lives. There are times when many of us wonder if it will ever quit us, even briefly, and give us some small space of relief.

If we are not afflicted in our bodies by arthritis or bursitis, beset by stomachaches or backaches or headaches or a hundred other ailments, we are prey to anxieties, frets and depressions that can drain joy from our lives.

Should we be so fortunate as to escape these afflictions of body and mind, we suffer in empathy with family and friends who are physically ill or undergoing mental distress. We are caught up with the wife agonizing over her husband who has been diagnosed as having cancer, with the mother sorrowing with her daughter who has lost a husband by an untimely death, with the parents grieving over an infant suddenly and frighteningly struck down by a mysterious illness.

I would suspect that for all of us there are times when we are minded to rip the telephone out of the wall and stuff it in a corner. We've reached a point where we feel we can't handle one more call announcing the death or hospitalization of one more friend or relative. As a long-suffering soul who is something of a wry wit remarked when we were discussing age and affliction: "Father, I rate a day as 'good' not when I have LESS trouble but one on which I hold my own and don't have any MORE trouble." Yes, it can get to be bad enough that we hope just to stay *even* with affliction. Just to hold our own!

In the light of this, there are some words we might call to mind which can provide, if not an easing of our afflictions, at least some consolation. From the Book of Exodus (2:11) in the Old Testament, there is this statement we can fix in our hearts: "I have surely seen the affliction of my people . . . and (I) have heard their cry . . . for I know their sorrows."

We are not alone in our affliction, nor is it an unattended thing. God knows and—what is so much more important—God cares. Proof that He cares is seen all through Exodus where God watched over His people. No less will be done for us.

In Christ, of course, we have incarnate the lesson on how to handle affliction. It is the doing of the will of Him who sent us also into this world to save others. Yes, He gives us the challenge: "Whoever wishes to be my follower must deny his very self, take up his cross each day, and follow in my steps" (Lk 9:23). Along with that challenge, however, He extends to us His comfort: "Come to me all you who labor and are burdened and I will refresh you" (Mt 11:28).

Above all, watching and learning Christ will help us

grasp this basic fact about affliction—we cannot be a crown-wearer, if we are not, first of all, a cross-bearer.

25   I Need the Cross

I was badly distracted the other morning while offering the Holy Sacrifice of the Mass. It was no ordinary distraction where my mind wandered over thoughts of what I'd have for breakfast or what I'd be doing for the rest of the day. The distraction came from the feast day I was celebrating and the Mass I was offering.

The feast was the Exaltation of the Holy Cross and the Mass, naturally, offered readings and prayers attuned to the theme of the day. Suddenly, I became aware that here was a feast that would be marked down by many as part of the "real old-fashioned" Church. Part of that Pre-Vatican II morbidity and fascination with spikes and crowns of thorns and that sort of thing. Enough horror and gore to make you shudder, you know.

Sadly, in many quarters, you do come upon such an attitude. It's mystifying to realize that for millions of Catholics, among all the things that have gone out of style, the Holy Cross rates high on the list of things best filed away and forgotten.

Oh, they will agree, that the Cross is there in the gospels and part of the Faith but we need not get lost in depressing concentration on wounds and blood and nails and thorns. Better that we substitute the resurrected Christ for the crucified one. It is certainly a lot easier on a queasy stomach to look on those crossed beams and see a radiant Jesus. Better that than the twisted corpus so beloved by that medieval mentality that has had too much influence on the Church these past centuries.

After all, they state, we are an *Easter* people not a Good Friday group. Christ did rise. Resurrection is our destiny. Why not celebrate that?

Well, believe me, I challenge none of that. *Why* should I? *How* could I? It is all so true. There is no one happier about resurrection as our destiny than I. I would dread to think that I have lived a life committed to Jesus Christ and His demands and find out that there was no destiny for me but a gaping hole in the ground after my life is completed.

At the same time, I do not want these exaggerated resurrectionists challenging me and my need to celebrate the crucified Christ.

Somehow or other, I do handle a toothache or a backache or any old ache, major or minor, in better fashion facing that crucified figure there before me. He tells me through his wounds and welts that he *KNOWS* what I suffer, that he can *USE* what I suffer, that I'll *MAKE* my own resurrection by what I suffer with and through Him.

There is no denying that faith in the Resurrection makes the prospect and the mystery of death less frightening. Faith in the Holy Cross, however, makes the immediate pains, sorrows and sufferings of life, those "slings of outrageous fortune," as Shakespeare calls them, more bearable and acceptable.

Celebrate as Easter people? Of course!

Somehow or other, though, I do not see how we can get to our Easter Sunday without an hour or two or even three of our own Good Friday. It's comforting to know that Christ proceeded that way and that He'll carry us through the same rite of passage to eternity.

26   Test of Fidelity

Of late years, I don't find myself running to pick up my mail as eagerly as I did when I was younger. Too often, the news it contains is not that good. Too many times, there is that letter telling me of the sickness or incapacitation of one of my senior friends. News of that sort always proves a "downer" for me as I recollect those good old days when these people were the young, vigorous, enthusiastic helpers with me in the Lord's vineyard.

Unrealistically, I keep telling God that none of them should be ill or disabled. He should permit them to continue on in their customary fine fettle, vital, thriving, striding through life like some "untouchable."

I'm sure God smiles tolerantly at my being so naive. How, He might ask, does one get to be grown-up without getting old and how does one get to be old without facing the aches, pains, buffetings and shocks of age?

How true it is! If we beg to GROW UP then we beg to GROW OLD. If we would see the high noon of our day then we must accept its dusk and sunset.

After a little chatting with the Lord along these lines and thinking things out, I turn to prayer; prayer for those who have been reported ill or disabled; prayer for those who are well that they remain so; prayer for all of us that no matter what condition God asks us to bear in our mature years, we are graced to do it IN HIM and WITH HIM and THROUGH HIM.

At any stage of our lives, *THAT* way of living is our true vocation. In childhood, in teen years, as middle-aged, or elderly, our call is living Christ and His way and truth and life. It is in our senior years, when, so often, the living gets to be a matter of suffering, that this Christian vocation becomes most important. Then, the suffering becomes almost like a final testing of our fidelity to the call we have heard and answered.

A prime charity that we can practice in our senior days is praying for our friends who are ill. Our petition should be that they meet this final testing with courage. Our prayer should be that they are able to say with St. Paul that "they have fought the good fight, they have run the course, they have finished the race."

It won't hurt, by the way, to add a petition for ourselves. No harm in asking that if, and when, our turn comes for a final testing, we are able to match all the valiant souls who have proved so faithful before us.

27   Four Great Fears

One of the most thought-provoking pieces I've come upon in the past year or so was a column written by Elmer Von Feldt in the Knights of Columbus magazine *Columbia*. Mr. Von Feldt wrote about the four great fears of man and showed how the Christian is equipped to face and overcome these fears throughout his life.

The four great fears are fear of failure, fear of rejection, fear of pain, and fear of death.

As we look at the listing of these fears, many of us haven't the slightest hesitation in assenting to the fact that we have been harried by them through most of our lives. From the time we have been children to the very moment we are reading these lines, the dread of rejection, or failure, or pain, or death, singly or in concert, has stalked us. We have gone to bed with them looming over us, waked and walked with them, fought them and fled them. Yet, they persist.

As we age, of course, the last two of the great fears often dominate our consciousness. They tend to cast their shadow over most everything we contemplate for our future. We, as Christians, have coped—and continue to cope—with them because we have been gifted by God with faith. We have words that not one, nor all of these fears, shall overcome us as long as we remain close to Him. His life instructs us, encourages us, sustains us in our coping.

If we fear failure and rejection, we have the solace of knowing that Christ suffered these fears more deeply and more desolatingly than we shall ever be asked to suffer them. His own people, the Jews, rejected Him and His call to them to believe He was their messiah. So depressed was He by rejection and failure among His people that Scripture tells us, He wept. What must have been the depth of his fear of rejection when, in his final hours, He heard the very people He had come to save, calling for his crucifixion?

Christ's fear of pain and death are highlighted for us by the evangelists as they describe that first Holy Thursday, Good Friday and Holy Saturday. Scripture tells us that He sweated blood in the Garden of Gethsemane just contemplating what was to happen to Him! Yes, He prayed THAT earnestly to be delivered from the passion and death that lay ahead.

The courage to conquer these fears is found for the Christian in the life of Christ. We should read that life, familiarize ourselves with the incidents that show us how Christ struggled as we do with fear of failure, rejection, pain and death.

In the learning and imitating of that life we are delivered from our own fears. Our constant prayer should be that Christ teach us how He did it that we may accomplish it by "learning of Him." As well, we should be thankful that God, through Christ, has delivered us from all our fears, great and small.

28 Dependency

I rate dependency on others as one of the great trials or crosses we seniors must bear as age takes its toll of us. It ranks right up there with those four great fears we reflected on previously. We might do well for the moment to take time out and consider this prospect of being forced by advancing years to depend on others for just about every aspect of our life from the necessity of getting about to the business of getting a bath.

As a help in this reflection, permit me to share with you some thoughts I wrote to a friend. They were in response to a letter in which she voiced her agony at the realization that she was no longer able to take care of herself. She had been shocked by her doctor's advice to find someone to look after her.

The following paragraphs hold essentially my answer to her in her dismayed state of mind:

"I've gone over your rather poignant letter on dependency more than a couple of times. The reason it touches me so deeply is that, as a writer, I have "lived" dependency many times in my vivid imagination. An author cannot but help cast himself in dozens of roles and, often, I have cast myself in that role—the old, feeble priest up on the second or third floor of a studentate being ministered to by young, ebullient, eager, vital, looking-toward-the-future seminarians.

"It so happens that I know this scenario well because I have been part of it. In my student days I was one of the seminarians who ministered to a couple of the older enfeebled priests who resided in our student house.

"Imagining *myself* now as the dependent one sends a chill down my spine, makes me groan to myself, and writhe a little. It sends me to my prie-dieu, or the side of my bed, or the chapel, to just about any old prayin' place handy, where I pray the prayer of the Garden. 'Father, if it be possible, let this chalice pass from me!' Grudgingly, I barely squeeze out my compliant: 'Not my will, but Thine be done.' But, that latter statement doesn't have a bit of my heart behind it. Though I say the words, I don't mean any of them.

"Thus, you see I have no trouble empathizing with the mood you evidenced in your letter but it would be foolish of me to pretend I had some message that would banish the mood. There is no simple or satisfying counsel, no quick-fix sentiment anyone can offer to make dependency acceptable.

"I can, however, share with you *what I do* when I play that frightening part of the old dependent padre. I call up some of the bitter things I have endured in life, recollect some of the heavy hurts, deep wounds, staggering disappointments, maddening frustrations suffered in trying to serve Christ in others. I fix my mind on one of these moments and its turmoil, the reluctance to suffer that I might have been going through at the time. I measure the moment against where I am now, and all that has transpired since then. Suddenly, I realize that Jesus and Mary *brought me through*. I was delivered by them through one more crisis, one more time. As other of life's trials and tribulations come to mind, I see that each was surmounted.

"No! No! this exercise *doesn't eliminate* my repugnance for the possibility of living old age totally dependent on

others. But the exercise does *renew my confidence* that, if and when dependency is my lot, *I will be brought through* one more crisis, one more time. There will be God's understanding and His Divine appreciation of my repugnance and there will be — as at all those other times — His graces to make it bearable."

I think any of us seniors who find ourselves fretting over dependency, or the prospect of it, might take some of these thoughts as a starting point toward learning to carry this cross. I don't say we will accept it very graciously because, as with myself, I suspect many of us will never accept dependency at all. We are too independent in our natures to change at this stage. But, a little thinking along these lines might help to make it bearable.

I don't think God will be displeased with us if we achieve that at least. And, as ever, He and Mary will bring us through one more crisis, one more time.

29   Aloneness Versus Loneliness — I

We don't need to take a poll of senior citizens to discover what is one of the leading grievances suffered by the elderly — loneliness. If this isn't the greatest burden of advanced years, it is never farther down on the chart of our dreads and fears than second or third. It is a prevalent bogey of the elderly. So much so, that many magazines and periodicals devoted to seniors and seniors' activities treat of loneliness almost on a regular basis.

The authors of the articles or studies usually end up indicating that loneliness must be recognized by us as more than a vague possibility in our future. With those near and

dear to us dying before us, with friends and neighbors passing away, or moving in with family, or entering nursing homes, our circle of loved ones gets narrower and narrower. By this simple process of nature taking its toll on our contemporaries — our aging friends and relatives — we are being left alone or being "made" alone.

Reality demands that we face it as a solid probability. The hard fact is simply this — that's life.

Once they have got us to accept this likelihood of loneliness in our lives, many discussants on the subject usually recommend that we be vigorous in doing something about dispelling it. Nature may be taking its toll on those close to us but nature cannot prevent *us* from pushing that narrowing circle closing in on us out to new and broader horizons.

We may lose family and friends in a variety of ways but we *can* make new associations, if we really and truly refuse to let this state of "aloneness" take over our lives. On the other hand, if we choose to sit and moan and brood over the condition, then *we* are choosing, basically, truly, to be lonely. It is *we*, not nature or life, who are keeping ourselves apart from people. It is *we* who are opting for this isolation that happens to so many of us as life thins out the ranks of family and friends.

For the moment, in this reflection, let's focus on the social remedying of this situation that is under our control. Apart from an incapacitation that prevents us from getting about, we can do something about aloneness. The first step in the plan is, of course, to make the firmest of resolves that we are going to break out of the narrowing world we have felt closing in on us.

From there on, other things should fall into place. We survey our circle of acquaintances, look about our neighborhood, investigate our church and we learn what activities are offered to seniors. We are going to discover that there are

lunches and dinners served, bus rides and pilgrimages scheduled, socials offered, lectures given, films presented — need I cover the roster of activities offered today for the senior in any city and in many parishes?

It is up to us to get involved. If we do, we will soon find that sense of aloneness that afflicts us being dissipated. We may even learn that there is a whole new world of friends out there ready, willing and able to fill our lives.

If we don't — if we won't — get involved, then we must cease our complaining. Let's be honest. If we do nothing about it, then being alone — suffering loneliness — is our responsibility. Simply, it's our own fault.

30   Aloneness Versus Loneliness — II

For a Catholic, loneliness should be no problem at all.

I realize that some may read that sentence and mutter that Father doesn't know what he's talking about. Believe me, every priest knows what he's talking about when he speaks about loneliness. His vocation chooses that condition for him right from the first day he is ordained.

True, his days may be filled with activities and functions and hundreds of people, but in and through all, he is ordained to be alone. When he goes to his room and shuts the door after the busiest of days, he has no one but himself to face. In the radical understanding of priesthood, ordination has made him a man without a family and friends. But, through his Mass and the Blessed Sacrament and his regular prayer life, he has God at hand, companioning him through the loneliest days and the emptiest nights.

BUT, every Catholic *has all that!* With Mass and the

Eucharist and prayer life, we are all called out of our loneliness to the companionship of Christ. With the Blessed Mother and her rosary, with the angels and the saints, we have a loving mother to look over us, we have guardians to protect us, we have brothers and sisters in heaven ready to heed us and our beckoning for companionship.

Fanciful nonsense? Sure, if you lack firm and vibrant belief. But, if you think with the mind of the Church and sense with the spirit of the Church and love with the heart of the Church, that previous paragraph is no fairy story. It is the reality of our Faith.

In the Eucharist, do we or do we not have the Real Presence, the body and blood, soul and divinity of Our Lord Jesus Christ? If we do, then we have a companion for all our days with whom, as the old song says, "We can walk and talk and tell our troubles to."

In each of the things mentioned above, we can go through the same exercise. They are or they are not true and efficacious. If they are, then we are not—we cannot be—alone. We can fill our lonely days with God, the Blessed Mother, the saints. We can read about them and learn about them until they are presences in our lives. We can fill our seemingly empty world with the best of companionship as we unite ourselves to them in prayer.

Granted, loneliness is the prospect for many of us but it can only remain a burden if we sit in it, stewing over it, doing nothing about it, socially or spiritually.

God does not intend that we suffer from being alone. He offers it as an opportunity on the spiritual side to come closer to Him, to have more of Him in our lives. On the social side, it is a chance to meet new friends, find new souls, do new things.

Through the happenstances of our growing old, nature may have rendered us alone. It cannot make us stay alone.

As we indicated in our first reflection on loneliness, only *we* can resist putting an end to our aloneness.

How foolish we are if we resist having God and His heavenly host plus our own newfound friends fill up our senior days.

31   On the Death of a Spouse

I have been treating of loneliness as something that can — and should — be dealt with summarily. Despite my urgings to the lonely that they become involved with other people or follow my encouragement to heighten their consciousness of God as a companion in their lives, I do not mean to minimize the problem it can present for us. A sense of loneliness can grip our hearts and minds and be resistant to our resolution to shake it off. It takes the most valiant efforts to overcome it. The operative words in that sentence are *valiant efforts*. Nothing less than this will help us succeed if we are among those afflicted by this cross.

One group of people in life who need the strongest support in making this valiant effort to overcome loneliness can be found among those who have suffered the loss of a spouse. Without belittling the loneliness any other people may feel through a loss in a family, nothing can equal the feeling of absolute aloneness a husband or wife feels at the death of a spouse.

The loss they suffer is almost in, and of, their very being. It is as if something of their body, soul and mind has been sundered from them and cast away. When we lose a mother, father, brother, sister or close friend, we have been separated from someone *outside* ourselves. Those who lose a

spouse have lost part of themselves. It is a violence done to their whole being. It comes close to affecting them in their very nature.

Scripture gives us the warrant for such a conclusion. Christ, in teaching His hearers about marriage, said: "Have you not read that God made them male and female and declared, 'For this reason a man shall leave his father and mother and cling to his wife and the two shall be one flesh'?" (Mt 19:4-5).

In the mystery of the sacrament of matrimony, the joining of the spouses is to make a unity, a oneness, a singleness. This is to be achieved for the fulfilling of God's — not man's — purpose. "Increase and multiply and fill the earth," says God to our first parents and, through them, to all parents that follow. It is His world, His sacrament, His way of bringing souls into the world to love Him, serve Him, and be happy with Him forever in eternity.

When the grace of the sacrament operates on this vowing of two people to be one, it is in God that they become one. They may not even realize it is happening to them and that it happens to them all the days of their marriage. Grace is operating not only to enable them to live together but also to sense together, feel together, work together and grow together. It may seem to be no substantiation of this argument on the depth of unity a man and a woman make in marriage, but I have often been amazed to see how much two spouses get to look like each other as they grow old! Could God be telling us something about this unity?

Since this union of two people is so powerful, since this bonding is so fast and intimate, since there is a reality about these two people becoming one, is it any wonder that when one partner dies, the other feels emptied out, adrift, lost? The suffering of aloneness can be so acute that it is almost destructive of their ability to function anymore.

Yet, all the suggestions I have made in the previous reflections hold for these people. They should be firm in resolving to overcome their feelings and find and make a new unity with others and with God.

Our obligation in charity is to help them make this new life. It is a charity we should willingly embrace. Especially should we help if we ourselves have suffered the loss of a spouse and have succeeded in achieving survival and the healing of the violence done us. We, above all, should share this knowledge of how we managed to find peace of soul and become reconciled to our loss.

All who suffer loneliness need our prayers and our support. Those who have lost a spouse, need it *most* of all.

32   Death and Dying

I don't remember anything about a story I once read except a tiny bit of dialogue one of the minor characters offered. I recall that the man was in prison and was sentenced to be shot as a spy. In reply to a cellmate's question on how he felt about his sentence, the prisoner replied, "It's not the dying that bothers me as much as death itself." I think I repeated the line to myself a couple of times because the sentiment impressed me so much.

The thought may not have the same impact for you that it had for me but, I must tell you, I found it was a powerful distinction the character made about one of life's great fears. Maybe, the reason I was so impressed is that whenever I think of the subject of death, the dying part seldom enters my mind. It is death itself that absorbs my thoughts.

Oh, of course, the how or where or when of dying

intrigues me as it does all of us. But it is not the thing that brings to my bones that little shudder, the small chill as when I contemplate death. To paraphrase the character from the forgotten story, I can say that it is not the business of dying that unsettles me, it is the matter of *being dead*.

I think if we do a little examining of our own responses, most of us would tend to agree that we all fundamentally feel this way. We realize that our picture of ourselves dying shows us as still *alive*. We may see ourselves as weak and near death perhaps, but in the scene, we are still struggling and *in* life. We know that while there's life, there's hope.

When we think of ourselves as dead, we know the finality of that condition. The struggling to stay alive is over. We have departed this world. An obituary notice will signal our world that we are no more.

We are dead.

Those three little words undoubtedly can shake our composure. As seniors, we have had enough experience of death to be aware of what it means to be dead. We have enough imagination to realize what it is that is over for us, what it is that is finished. Gone is the rising to a bright new day or the warmth of affection from friends or the enjoyment of rapturous music; gone are all the sights and sounds and sensations of the world we have been a vital part of, possibly shaped and, certainly, been shaped by. We will never again experience it or enjoy it or share it with someone we love. Never again.

Beyond the awfulness of this realization lies the more shattering one. In death, what have we gone to? Dust, oblivion, annihilation? Is our eternal tomorrow the nothingness preached by the atheist or the skeptic?

Our faith's resounding answer is "No!" Our destiny is an eternal life besides which this life will be seen to pall. St. Paul tells us that eye has not seen, nor ear heard, the glory,

the wonder, the beatitude that awaits us when we are united with God the Father, the Son and the Holy Spirit. Christ risen is prelude to our rising, to be happy forever in heaven.

Heaven, and a mansion that He has prepared for us in His Father's house, is Christ's promise to us after we die. It is this promise that lifts from us the chilling effect that thoughts of death and dying might have upon us.

True, it isn't — it has never been — easy for man to face into his death. Since Adam and Eve, all their children and their children's children have studied, experimented, dreamed of ways to escape the burden of mortality. No one has ever achieved success in avoiding it. It is unlikely that anyone ever will, because as Scripture tells us, "It is appointed once for man to die" (Heb 9:27).

As Christians we believe in the beautiful words of the Mass for the Deceased that "life is changed, not taken away." This faith is what helps us to escape from the fear of death. All the promises we have from Christ are that we move to a new plane of living. We enter into eternity and beatitude forever in His presence before the throne of God.

How many and how wonderful are the words of Christ who tells us that He came that we might have life everlasting.

Nothing less than this is our destiny!

So — if we brood about our life's coming to an end, if we feel that little chill when reflecting on our dying and our being dead, it is time to meditate on the *coming* of Christ rather than on our *going*. "I have come that you may have life and have it more abundantly" (Jn 10:10).

We do not "pass away" (as the euphemism used by so many today describes death). In a manner of speaking, we don't even die. We pass to a new life in God through

Christ. Joining the Blessed Mother, all the angels and saints, our own dear mother and father, all our beloved friends and relatives, we enjoy happiness in heaven forever.

When you consider all this, there is hardly anything at all to dread about death, is there?

Virtue

"It is not enough to know about
  virtue, then, but we must endeavor
  to possess it, and to use it."

Aristotle

33   What Ever Happened to Virtue?

I have no resources for tracking through history and finding
out if there was ever an age that equaled ours for its interest
in and endorsement of personal betterment. I need no
resources to know that if any age equaled us in this enthusiasm, it did not surpass us!

The most cursory glance at a magazine or a daily newspaper, only a few hours listening to the radio, a day spent
with a television set, provide us with a veritable encyclopedia
of counsel on self-improvement.

Unctuous voices with earnest tones deliver insistent
spiels in which they cajole, beg, demand that we develop
slimmer figures, or clearer skin, or healthier hair, or bright-
er teeth. We are exhorted to become smoother dancers, or
better pudding makers, or facile conversationalists, or
fluent letter writers. Nothing escapes the hortatory mes-
sages that are highlighted or blared at us in any or all forms
of the media as we are told to sharpen our wits, shape our
bodies, hone our skills, polish up our manners. The message
comes at us, loud and clear. Improve! Improve! Improve!

But one looks in vain for any exhortation toward betterment of our souls. With the emphasis on the improvement
of the body or of our social talents and graces or of our
minds, you would get the impression that for many of these

people who are offering products and services, the soul doesn't count. As a matter of fact, for too many of them, the soul doesn't exist!

The absolute lack of any encouragement toward holiness of life can be almost depressing. No wonder we are tempted at times to cry out: "Never mind the body and avoiding cholesterol and fat and sugar; never mind being a better dancer or cook or conversationalist. How about just being a better person? What about goodness? What ever happened to the practice of virtue?"

From the world I've described it is obvious that we cannot look to our society to care about holiness of life.

The burden of advancing that cause falls squarely upon us.

As Our Lord said: "So let your light shine before men, that they may see your good deeds and give praise to your heavenly Father" (Mt 5:16). Thus, we cannot let ourselves be discouraged or depressed with the world's concentration on the body and its ignoring of the spirit.

It is our vocation, through our words and by our actions, to show the world that virtue is alive and well and thriving. It should be shining forth in *our* souls as we fulfill Christ's commands and counsels to be perfect as our heavenly Father is perfect.

For all the world to see, we are to follow Christ's example — to learn of Him — to imitate Him as we strive to live a life filled with virtue.

34 Seek the Virtue of Wisdom

One of my favorite little magazines is a publication titled: *God's Word Today*. It is a monthly pamphlet devoted to a study of some special section or book of Scripture. A short reading from the Scripture section under study is assigned daily. Books from both the Old and the New Testament are covered in the course of the year.

One of the recent issues centered on the Book of Wisdom from the Old Testament. I tell you, any man or woman who has trouble finding a thought to meditate or reflect upon need only take up this book of the Bible. In it, they will find a lifetime of themes and may well come to their last moments still not having exhausted the depth of thought contained in the chapters of Wisdom.

My deep interest in it comes because I have always considered the virtue of wisdom as one of the choicest to possess. No matter what your state or age, I cannot urge you too strongly, too fervently, to petition God for your full share of this grace.

Spiritual writers tell us that with wisdom we come to an understanding of the acts and dispositions of God toward His children. *Here* is the core of wisdom's efficacy — through the possessing of this virtue, we come to *appreciate* fully God's judgments for ourselves and our world.

What a blessing, then, to possess wisdom in our lives! Who of us has not been shaken, unsettled, by events in the world that, in our viewing, are outrageous and make no sense? War, murder, hostage-taking, brutality, famine, flood, drought, earthquake, tornado — these devastating occurrences in society and nature leave us reeling and confused. We are unable to understand the place and the meaning of these scourges laid across the back of mankind.

Our personal lives often present no better or easier circumstances to help clarify the mystery of God's operation. Few of us can claim that we have never felt alienated, hurt, resentful toward God because of seemingly inexplicable situations in which He has placed us and from which we have suffered deeply. Then, too, we experience shocking, seemingly senseless deaths, illnesses, traumas and tragedies in our families. We can make no whole from these oddly cut pieces of a puzzle God seems to be making us live.

Possessing the virtue of wisdom helps give some scope and some deeper, broader vision of what is going on in our world and in our lives. Of course, not immediately! It is not as if we can snap on a mental light switch and the darkness in our mind is suddenly and fully illuminated. Achieving wisdom takes time but it is worth all the effort we extend to possess it.

With wisdom, what have seemed the disjointed, the irregular, the capricious events of our life and the lives of those around us are grasped as having place and purpose. Life has been compared by one of the poets to the weaving of a tapestry. In the weaving, he wrote, we see only the underside of what is being woven. With wisdom, our vision becomes broader and we begin to see what God sees — the overside of the tapestry and the pattern being made.

If you ever begged God for anything, beg for the virtue of wisdom.

What could equal possessing the grace to see things more nearly *as God sees them?*

35   The Best of Habits — Reading the Bible

Far and away, the all-time best seller among all the books EVER printed is the Bible. Even today, in a culture that is labeled secular and humanistic, sales of the Bible continue to register strong and steady. The Bible outsells, yearly, many of the highly promoted works that make it to the best-seller list.

People have often joked about this boast for the Bible and its outselling of all other books. The most frequent comment is the cynical one that "the Bible is the best sold and the least read book in the history of publishing."

I have no way of proving that sarcastic remark true or untrue. I'm inclined to lean toward the opinion that it is false. Best seller or not, the Bible, I would contend, is one of our more frequently read books. Granted, much of the reading is vicarious. We participate in a service or ceremony and listen as someone else reads the Scripture assigned for the day or the occasion. Nonetheless, we are attending to the readings and are aware of the importance of the word of God being brought into our lives.

The trouble with such a procedure, however, is that too many allow this vicarious contact with the Bible to supply for their own need to take up the word of the Lord and read, ponder and pray. Under these circumstances of benign neglect, the cynic's remark is truly and sadly accurate. The Bible can become the least read of all the books ever published. It has been read too often *for* us and *to* us.

These readings at which we are spectators or audience are really meant to stimulate us to go to the book itself and continue reading. They are teasers, appetite whetters.

Hearing the Scriptures read is a blessed and salutary practice but *reading* it ourselves is more efficacious.

I cannot too strongly urge all of us, now, in these senior years to make daily Scripture reading a habit. If we do not have a Bible handy in our home or apartment, we should get one immediately. I recommend that we start our reading with the New Testament. Here, until we have matured in our appreciation of the Scriptures, we will be on familiar ground. Much of the reading will evoke recollections of the times we have heard a parable or passage before. The names and places, the stories surrounding Christ's preaching and miracles will have a familiar ring. It will be easier to develop our habit of reading the Bible by starting on this familiar ground.

Set aside some part of each day for the reading. For example, do it right after breakfast or in the evening before retiring but try to do it regularly at the same time each day. I recommend this procedure because such a practice will develop your Bible reading into a habitual thing. This is what we want Scripture reading to be for us — a habit of life.

At the beginning, don't attempt to read too much Scripture at any one time. We should set ourselves some limit, say, twenty verses of whatever book of the Bible we are reading. Once finished, we should mark the place, say a prayer, take a moment for reflection on the passage and how it affects our life, and put the book aside.

We will be surprised how swiftly we find ourselves moving through the books of the New Testament. More, we will be delighted at the insights we are getting into the life of Jesus Christ and His days on earth among men. Our appreciation of the sameness of peoples' resistance to Christ's message will grow. We will see that people are the same in any age where God exacts a standard of life for them. And, we will find ourselves glaringly apparent in many of the

stories and incidents that Christ uses to teach people what He means for them to do to be saved.

No book we ever touch will teach us as much as the Bible. If up to now it has been for us no more than that great untouched masterpiece of literature — change that — start making the Bible a daily companion.

It is after all our map of sanctity and salvation. We should make it a habit to study that map regularly to keep ourselves sure of the Way, the Truth and the Life.

36   Scrambling the Saints

Of the many things that have caused me some grievance in this age of the renewed Church, one, in particular, has been most vexing. It is what I call the game of Scrambling the Saints.

I have never read a good explanation for the seemingly (in so many cases) arbitrary shuffling of the feast days of the Lord's holy women and men. Why some dear saint of mine must be yanked from a summer date and dropped into a winter cycle or vice versa, escapes me. Why, for example, St. Thomas Aquinas had to be moved from March 7 to January 28, or St. Alphonsus Liguori shifted from August 2 to August 1, or St. Dominic shuffled from August 4 to August 8, has never been too clear to me. More mysterious is why some saints have been jammed into each other's feast day as happened to Timothy and Titus. And, why another saint, such as St. Andrew Corsini, is dropped entirely, goes beyond the comprehension of my limited intellect.

It was this latter situation from which I suffered the worst blow in this juggling and jettisoning of saints. When I

came to celebrate my birthdate the first year that the new calendar was in use, I found that my "second" name saint, Andrew Corsini, had been unceremoniously dropped from the roster of the blessed!

How my dear old paternal grandmother must have grieved when that excision took place! Staunchly she had fought my father right up to the baptismal font to have me named Andrew after the good saint on whose feast day I had been born. Her persistence had come close to wrecking the christening party planned by the clan. The dear woman could have saved herself the crisis. Our modern saint-minders took care of any problem she might have had. They unceremoniously dumped Andrew out of the calendar.

I rate the procedure of shifting, suppressing, omitting, deleting, abandoning the saints and their feast days as a mistake. It is what we might describe as a poor judgment call on the part of those responsible for the new roster of saints.

True, the list needed to be cleaned up. Granted, there were saints of dubious date and data. Notwithstanding, the legitimate saints, the traditional men and women who had attained the beatific vision might better have been left alone. I fail to see where renewal has been advanced an inch by scrambling these faithful stewards of the Master.

I add one further — and most important — consideration. If there is one thing our young people could use today, it is a great bath, a saturation, in the lives of the saints. Considering the staggering failure today — on all levels of our society — of our leadership, the young could use these heroes and heroines of Christ to inspire them with much needed ideals. When we contemplate the abysmal lack, in our age, of true and exciting role models in spirituality for the young, it is outrageous to think we have compounded the problem by this current denigration of saints and saint-

hood as revealed through our Church calendar. It is subtle denigration — but, it is there.

Somehow, I don't think Christ has done any casting away and shuffling about of these loyal souls who served Him so well in their lifetimes. I am sure they continue *close* and *dear* to Him.

If they are cherished by Him, that's good enough for me. Whether they are in or out of the Church calendar I am most happy to have His friends as my friends.

Need I exhort you to continue your own devotions to your favorite saints? Read about them, meditate on their lives, imitate them, don't be embarrassed by them.

And, above all, tell others — especially the young — about them. They need them.

37   Wanted: True Heroes and Heroines

I get the impression while watching TV these days that many moderns must find their lives absolutely, staggeringly boring. A reading of the daily newspaper only confirms this suspicion that so many, in fact, too many people in our time must live the dullest of lives with one drab day following upon the other.

If there is any doubt about my suspicion that many lead these dull-as-dishwater lives, it evaporates as I count the number of talk shows that fill the TV schedules through the average day. Hour after hour of any day, the TV tube presents the jet-setters or their playmates, the glamorous folk of radio, TV and films.

What bolsters this conviction about our world's being bored with itself is the volume of gossip and scandal columns carried by our newspapers and magazines. We seem entranced by what all these "super" people, these media darlings, are eating, wearing, drinking, doing and not doing.

I know that some might counter my charge and say that this situation has always been part of any society. All ages have had their curiosity about the rich or the royal, the famous or the notorious folk in their society. It is no more than that human propensity to know "how the other half lives." In a basic way, it is no more than expressing our need to have heroes and heroines, worthy or not, who represent certain ideals and values after which we yearn and toward which we strive.

If I grant that, then, I am left with the sad notion that we have come to a sorry state if these media darlings represent ideals and values that fill our dreams and motivate our drive toward excellence in life. More to the point, may God help the young if this is the best we can do for them in presenting personal goals for which they should aim.

Sadly, as Catholics, we do no better for our youth than do the secularists who control and influence so much of our life and culture. In our previous reflection, I mentioned that we have done badly by the saints. In all but ending the importance of Mary and the saints in our liturgy, we've deprived our youngsters, as Christians (which they are by the call of Christ and baptism, first, last and always), of their true heroes and heroines.

Such deprivation has left them with this world's so-called "great" souls. What models we offer them! A collection of greedy, vain, shallow, insecure, inept, spiritually deprived, media-made and media-hyped men and women who are as insubstantial and unreal as the characters they mime on the stage or TV or films.

I think it's time that we who know the importance of the saints in our world, we who have read about them and imitated them and envied them their place with God, mount a campaign to reassert their importance in our Church.

Our young Catholics need these true idealists who followed Christ. There is no ideal that the world can offer that matches that vocation. Certainly, there is no ideal the world can offer more guaranteed to keep life from being boring than the following of Christ — for us or for our young people.

And, just in case any of us might chance to be among the bored, among those who are finding days dull and drab, give this ideal a try.

You'd be amazed how "unboring" life can become at any age trying to live up to the ideal of following Christ.

38 Hold That Judgment

The following snatch of poetry I share with you is a fairly ancient piece. It was written by Francis Quarles (1592-1644), an English poet. Though three hundred years plus separate us from the author, his advice is the sort that is ever-timely. It fits the people of any place and any century.

> My soul,
> Sit thou a patient looker-on;
> Judge not the play before the play is done;
> Her plot has many changes;
> Every day speaks a new scene;
> The last act crowns the play.

How true this counsel would have been to anyone who was an onlooker at the time of Christ and watched His three years of public life. How often, as the crowds walked away from Christ, or challenged His teaching, or picked up stones to hurl at Him, might the onlooker have been tempted to say: "This fellow is wasting his time. He's getting nowhere with these people."

Imagine his reaction as he stood in the crowd on Calvary and saw the agony and death of Christ between two thieves. "He's an abject failure," the observer might mutter as he left the hill and strolled home. "So much for the wonder-worker of Nazareth."

Sadly, for the onlooker, he had judged the play too soon. He should have waited to see the last act of this drama being played out on the following Sunday when Christ rose from the dead. Christ crowned the "play" with His greatest miracle — the Resurrection!

Not all lessons are as obvious in life as this one, are they? But we do see with some immediacy from this example from Christ's life that if we have a tendency to judge too quickly anyone's life, we are unfair to them and foolish in such precipitancy. Who can tell how a person will crown the play they write with their daily living? Odd as that life may seem to us, fruitless, worldly, even vicious or evil, who can tell what the final curtain may bring?

Recall, again, the scene on Calvary. As an onlooker, we might have condemned the Good Thief long before he was crucified along with Christ. A wastrel, a brigand, a mugger, we might have felt justified and content to see that he was going to get his due as he struggled with his cross to Calvary. What a shock to us to hear Christ promise him paradise THAT DAY!

I think we would all agree this is a lesson well taken. Before judging others — give pause and remember the final

line of Francis Quarles' poem: "The last act crowns the play."

39   The Young Teach Me a Lesson

On two successive weekends recently, I had occasion to be involved with two sets of young "hopefuls." On one Saturday, I was invited to officiate at the wedding of a young cousin and his bride. Then the Saturday that followed, I was part of a celebration of seven novices as they committed themselves by their vows to the religious life.

Both occasions were an inspiration. To accept the vows of a young couple as they pledge to love, honor and obey each other until death do us part, cannot help but lift a man's spirits. Then, to witness the vows of seven novices as they pledge to serve God in Poverty, Chastity and Obedience cannot help but make a man examine his attitude about the younger generation.

Too often these days, I must admit, I find myself critical of young people. Almost instinctively, when I see a group of youngsters my mind is flooded with negatives. I judge them as too loud, too silly, too selfish, too pushy and disrespectful. I don't know any of the youngsters, I have absolutely no right to be critical, but I find I am.

These two occasions of which I write have me striking my breast in contrition. In those weekends I met young souls who are every bit as solid as any I recall from my own younger days. Their devoutness and purpose as they entered marriage and the religious life was inspiring. They prove that I am wrong in my hasty assessment of this gen-

eration. They indicate that this "old dog" had better "learn new tricks."

I pray that these reflections of mine strike a chord in any of us who are as guilty as I of harshly judging today's young people. We could all well take a little time and examine our conscience. Do we find we judge too quickly and too severely the young people with whom we come into contact? If our answer is "Yes," then join me in working on a change of heart.

Remember, the young people are aware of our attitude. They sense our severity in judging them. We don't have to say a word. Our disapproval is often fairly obvious as we deal with them and are impatient, curt, summary.

It won't hurt us — and it certainly will benefit the youngsters — if we learn to be more temperate in our response to them.

Let's give these juniors what we seniors asked for ourselves in our young days — a chance to prove ourselves.

40   Resolution — The Grade A Kind

In the early years of my priesthood, at the end of my annual retreat, I found usually that I had a notebook full of significant quotes from the retreat master. Along with that, I found I had what amounted to almost another half notebook of resolutions to be put into effect after the retreat.

More times than I care to admit, the next year, as I prepared for retreat, I would dig out the retreat notebook of the year past and find, neatly packed with it, those great resolutions I had fashioned. The latter were all shiny and

bright like newly minted coins. My resolutions showed not the slightest bit of wear or tarnish. They could have been described as well-kept, if you mean secreted, hidden away.

But, they had hardly been well-kept, if we consider why I made them in the first place. They were made to be acted upon. They were to be incorporated into the regimen I was to follow to achieve the perfection God asked of me — the pursuit of "being perfect as your heavenly Father is perfect."

There is a laughable (I almost wrote the word *pathetic* there) aspect to all this. Even after reviewing this yearly proof of the lack of solid purpose on my part, at the end of the new retreat, I would have another half notebook of fresh resolutions!

I estimate that it took me about seven years to wise up to my stupidity. I was making resolutions merely for the sake of making resolutions. In the light of my burying them year after year until time for the next retreat, there was no other explanation for my action. Once I faced into this contradiction I was perpetrating, I stopped making resolutions on my retreats.

Please note — I did not say I stopped *resolving*.

The change in what I did was merely a matter of simplification and focus. I sought out the worst of my faults, the weakest of my weaknesses, and fixed on that. *That* became the subject of my retreat prayers and meditations and the issue on which I spent time in my retreat confession.

At the end of the retreat, I made my single resolution on that particular fault or weakness. I wrote it down, BUT did not put it away with the retreat notebook. I put it in my Breviary — the priest's prayer book for his recitation of the Divine Office. Seeing the resolution, day after day, and each time every day that I picked up the Breviary to recite the Office, I was able to concentrate on the resolution. I made it

into what one old retreat master I knew used to describe as a "Grade A Resolution."

Over the past pages we have shared a sufficiency of recommendations and urgings about things to practice, to do, to be involved in, to make part of our senior living. Would it shock anyone for me to say please don't make any resolutions on them?

Note again — I did not say *stop resolving*.

Resolve we must but don't waste time learning the hard way that success in the development of our spirituality is effected by simplifying our purpose. Learn from my own experience to concentrate on making and keeping *one* resolve.

If there is a glaring weakness in self that needs to be overcome, then make that the target of prayer and penance. Persist in going after it and not after something else that is of little consequence toward improving our spirituality.

From all we have reflected on in these pages, some one devotion, practice, fault, problem, idea should stand forth as *THE* thing we should be working for, or on, to make ourselves holy and more pleasing to God.

That one thing should be the object of our "Grade A Resolution." It is to be written down, seen each day, reviewed each night, persisted in until we possess the virtue or devotion or no longer indulge the weakness or fault.

If we succeed in living *one* "Grade A Resolution" a year you can be sure that nothing less than a Grade A life will be ours.

41 "The Good That I Would, I Do Not"

The words of St. Paul that give us the title for our reflection might seem to be a terribly depressing expression of futility in any efforts we might attempt to improve our lives. A glance at the title might have us asking: What's the use of trying? Let's suppose we purpose for ourselves a course of good actions and make, as has been recommended, that *Grade-A Resolution*. To be told we face into a situation where the good we would, we'll end up not doing, seems to indicate that we'll end up wasting precious time. The resolution will prove to have been in vain.

Admittedly, that is one way of taking St. Paul's words. It is not the correct way. St. Paul was writing not to depress us but to encourage us. He was bringing our attention to the reality of self and the weakness of self that is involved so frequently in pursuing a life of holiness and perfection. This is possibly the most important reality to grasp when we essay the higher, the better, the more perfect life.

One thing that is common to all the saints as we study their lives is the fact that they are eminently and above all things, realists. They took nothing for granted about their fallibility and weakness. They were only too well aware of the drag of the flesh against the spirit.

As we read life after life of these holy men and women of God we might be surprised at the insistence and the unceasingness of their prayers begging God to prevent them from quitting the pledge they had made to follow Him. I think the first time I came upon such a plea in the life of St. Teresa of Avila (whose biography I was reading) I smiled and thought, she has to be kidding, considering the sufferings she has undergone. But, a few years added to my life and a few hard bumps in my personal effort to achieve

perfection, wiped that smile from my face. I could understand the saint's prayer after a few failures humbled me.

The saints *knew* themselves. They knew that all the good they would do, they frequently didn't do. And they were always honest about recognizing the weakness that impeded accomplishing the good intended. They knew the meaning of the Scripture expression that "pride goeth before the fall."

Our own efforts toward a spiritual life in these our senior years will be persevered in more zealously if we get basic. Be a realist as were the saints. If we have a lifetime of indulgence in a bad habit or some vice, a mere resolve to eliminate this obstacle to our salvation is not going to do the trick. We are going to face temptations, as St. Paul's words indicate, and we are going to fail. *Above all*, be prepared to fail. Be prepared to recognize that the good we would, we often won't do. Not because we are perverse but because we are weak.

BUT, St. Paul was not encouraging us to chuck the whole business of trying to be a better person because of a failure. He was indicating that we humble ourselves, place more of our dependence on God, get back to the resolution, and pursue it once more.

It is from St. Paul, as well, that we gain an insight into how success comes when we are struggling to be good. He had begged God to relieve him from a trial he describes as a "sting of the flesh." Three times, he tells us, he begged the Lord for deliverance from the burden. And three times, God's answer was that he must carry this weakness but he must have confidence it could be managed. God's promise was: "My grace is sufficient for you" (2 Cor 12:9).

So, too, it will often be with us in this pursuit of spirituality. Some fault from which we would dearly love to be delivered — a sharp tongue, impurity, uncharitableness,

sloth — we will be asked to carry as our cross. Being realistic, we will know that *alone* we cannot do it. The good that we would, we will not be doing — and won't get done — UNLESS we go in humility to God and His Blessed Mother and ask for the graces needed to do the good we would.

His grace will come.

His grace will be sufficient for us.

Seasonal Thoughts

To everything there is a season,
and a time to every purpose under
the sun.

Ecclesiastes 3:1

42   Thanks for What?

It's interesting how some experiences in life make no impression on us at all and disappear from our minds almost immediately after they occur. Then, there are others, seemingly no more significant, that strike us powerfully and are, as people say, etched on our memory, never to be forgotten.

About a year ago, I was visiting patients in a hospital and walked into a room where I thought an aunt of mine had been placed. It was obvious as I stared at the burly, rather discontented looking man in the bed that I had goofed on the room number. He seemed to have a half dozen intravenous bottles around the head of his bed and tubing from them running into his arms and legs from every direction. I exaggerate, of course, but in the embarrassment over the error about my aunt, I was not being very precise in my observing of things.

Curtly, he told me that my aunt had been moved to another floor. I thanked him but delayed a moment, thinking I'd exchange a few pleasantries and then go about my business. The Thanksgiving holiday was due in a week and I remarked that I hoped he wouldn't have to remain in the hospital over the holiday. "I hope you're out and able to celebrate Thanksgiving with your family."

His lips curled cynically and he indicated his arms that

looked as if he were undergoing acupuncture rather than IV feeding. "Thanksgiving for what?"

I didn't have any glib answer. "Well, enjoy the holiday, anyway," I said and headed out to find my aunt.

Of course — later on — back in the rectory, I thought of all kinds of neat things I should have said to him. Sadly, the opportunity had passed to communicate my thoughts to the irate man I chanced on. Yet, they may have validity for some of us elders, so why don't I share them?

It is not at all inconceivable that to any one of us who might be plagued by sickness, giving thanks is the last thing we might think of. Fretted and wearied by a host of ills and ailments that could keep a clinic going night and day, thanksgiving would not have a high place on our list of priorities. And who could argue with us, especially if we are suffering a crushing sickness that permits no respite and for which there is no promise of a cure?

Yet, in fairness, we might remind ourselves that life was not always thus. God may be making us carry a burden now but there were those days when we were asked to shoulder nothing of the weight of Christ's cross. Letting the past flash through our mind we must admit that there were those days filled with pleasure and joys. There were the happy days, exciting days, days crammed with love and affection, days that saw us enjoying the satisfaction of success in marriage or business or a career. God gave us all these pleasures and joys, even as now He asks the bearing and the sharing of some of His cross.

Oh! How I wish I had delayed and said all this to my surly friend in the hospital! Yet, these reflections might be something we all can keep for reference. Should the day come when we are tempted to refuse to thank God for NOW, we might remember some of the past and thank Him for all the wonderful THENS.

No matter how desperate and depressing things get, we must never forget that God gave us all the good times as well. And, if the truth were to be told, I'll bet that a matchup of the good times versus the bad times shows that the former far outweigh the latter.

Thanksgiving for what?

Thanksgiving for *that*!

43   Just Another Advent

I don't know if you have ever spent much time in studying the calendar of the Church year. Do it sometime. You will find it is a beautiful and remarkable device for jolting us from any of the spiritual ruts into which we may have fallen as the year moves on. Just as the changes in nature's seasons alert us to the need to change gears in our mode of living, so too the seasonal shifts in the Church's calendar alert us to shift gears in our mode of spirituality.

In nature, for example, as autumn comes on, we sense that the easy living of summer is finished and that winter is just over the next hill. We ready our homes for the icy blasts that will seek out the openings around windows and doors. Up go the storm windows and on goes the caulking compound for the house. We want to make sure that we fill even the tiniest crack to prevent losing that precious heat that is so expensive to come by these days. Next, we lay up a store of rock salt for sprinkling on the icy walks. Finally, we check to be sure that the old faithful snow shovel, the warm heavy gloves and the trusty boots are positioned for handy use when, and if, Mr. Winter comes on with the big snow.

The Church and her calendar prove no less vigilant in

making us attentive to seasonal changes for the soul. No great feast, no special Church devotion, no sacred time comes upon us unannounced and as some great surprise. Could anyone ever complain that the Church doesn't give us fair warning at the approach of Easter or Christmas, of the coming of Pentecost, or the arrival of the stirring feasts of Christ and Mary?

A good example of what I'm writing about comes to mind at the moment as I stare at a box of Christmas cards on my desk. We are in the season of Advent. The place of Christmas in our lives is no surprise to us if we have been heeding the Church calendar. For four consecutive Sundays we are told of the approach of the beautiful feast of Christ's birth. We are exhorted through psalms, readings, hymns and prayers to ready ourselves, become worthy, dispose our souls for celebrating the anniversary of the birth of Christ.

If we accept Advent casually, the feast could be old hat to us, nothing to get excited about, something seen and gone through many, many times before.

Don't fall into the trap of feeling you've seen it all before. Remember, the Church signals us through her calendar to ready ourselves to be worthy to receive Christ.

The calendar doesn't say a thing about old age excluding us from the need to prepare.

If anything, we should be "ready-er" than most people for the coming of Christ and Christmas. After all, having enjoyed these extra years and come to seniority, we've had more chance than others to practice getting ready.

44 Christmas and the Poor Souls

Preaching offers many challenges to a priest in his lifetime. They can come from a host of sources, the most obvious source being the congregation. I think I could do a book on the occasions when someone in the audience decided, as the famed comedian Jimmy Durante used to describe it, "to get into the act."

They do not necessarily want to get into the preacher's act, though I have had interrupters and contradictors jump up during a talk and shout out their challenges. Sometimes the person goes into his own performance from singing a song to determining that the sermon time is a good one for making the Stations of the Cross. On one occasion, I recall a lady ostentatiously striding up the center aisle to light all the unlighted candles on the vigil light stands and dropping coin after coin in the offering boxes. The clink upon clink of the money was not much help in getting across a stirring message to the faithful.

But, the challenge that has often fascinated me is the matter of the subjects you are asked to preach on by the group to which you may be preaching. These, believe me, can range from the lives of the saints to why the President isn't doing more to increase social security payments for senior citizens.

Our title at the head of this reflection comes from just such a situation. It was the end of November and I was finishing up a novena to the Poor Souls as Advent began. Someone asked if I would say a few words about the Faithful Departed and Christmas. The conjunction of the two subjects had never occurred to me but the more I thought about them, the more I realized how well they fit together.

True, the subjects swing between two extremes of emo-

tion. November, a month dedicated to the Poor Souls, finds us somber and reflective as we are reminded of life after death and of our dear departed who have gone before us. On the other side, when December takes the stage, we are pulled toward the ascent of that peak of joy so associated with Christmas and the birth of our Savior.

Yet, with a little reflection, we see that there is no problem in mixing and matching these two phases of our Faith. In fact, in a fitting way, we realize that Christmas and the Poor Souls belong together.

Who better than the Faithful Departed know the full meaning of waiting for the coming of Christ? Like the Jews of old, the Poor Souls know the poignant yearning for Christ to deliver them. Then, in their deliverance from purgatory, they experience the purpose and the power of Christmas — salvation and union with God in heaven.

These thoughts should be an occasion for joy on our own part even while we may still mourn the loss of our loved ones. What consolation for us to realize that while we struggle to appreciate what Christ did for us, while we strain to grasp this mystery of His birth, our loved ones who have died know *now* the meaning of Christmas.

Were they back with us today, we could not give them such a gift even were we to wrap up the whole wide world and put it under the Christmas tree for them.

These thoughts have proved a comfort to me often since the first day I received the challenging subject to talk on. I'm glad the retreatants put me to the test. What more consoling thought on our Poor Souls do we need than the knowledge that they enjoy Christmas now as they never did on earth?

May God be glorified in their everlasting joy and their sharing with Him an everlasting Christmas!

45   Lent Lasts a Lifetime

To say that Lent lasts a lifetime is an obvious contradiction of the calendar of the liturgical year. Even a tot struggling with her first CCD assignment knows better than that. Upon questioning her, I'm sure we would be informed quite definitely by said tot: "Lent lasts for forty days, no more, no less."

Why, then, do I state that it lasts a lifetime? Well, because, basically, there is *Lent* and, then, there *is* Lent. There is the one that covers about seven weeks on the spring calendar. It is a period of time marked out between Ash Wednesday and Easter Sunday. Then there is the one that might be described as a way of life. This is the Lent that, in its lessons, its challenge, its demands and its pervading influence on us, lasts a lifetime. It is a period of time marked out between the cradle and the grave.

Sometimes I think it is too bad that we learn and can recite so well the fact that Lent lasts forty days. I think this has caused some of us to gear ourselves to "live up" to being good Catholics and Christians for that period. Comes Easter Monday, we feel, somehow, that we can lower our sights on the pursuit of virtue and sanctity for the other 325 days of the year.

Of course, "living up" to Lent is much better than someone saying, as Lent approaches, "Oh, well, just another Lent." Too many, with those casual words and that casual attitude, let the season slip by without another thought of its importance and significance.

How sad, we might comment, that anyone would let the season go to waste. But, let me offer a caution. Waste of a sort could be going on in our lives too. How sad if the marking of the many Lents we have lived has not taught us

the great lesson of the season — true happiness is found in the denial of self and the affirmation of God in our lives.

Now, do you see why I remarked, as we began this reflection, that Lent lasts a lifetime? When are we ever quit of this search to be happy with Christ and, thus, when are we ever quit of the need to learn the lesson of self-denial and commitment to God by which it is ultimately achieved?

Lent is the time in which we have the opportunity to examine ourselves. A time to judge how well we are living the true following of Christ — the emptying of self, the denying of self, the giving of self. It is a time to sharpen our practice of this demand of discipleship in Christ. "If you would be my disciple, go, sell all you have and give to the poor, and come follow me."

Once we have got this rule of discipleship in proper perspective, the true practice of Lent asks that we make a resolution. We are asked to resolve to live the high ideal we may have been falling short of.

Sure, it is a difficult and testing kind of practice. But, it is what we are called to by Christ as he urges us, "Come, follow me." Our consolation is in knowing that He walks with us. He does not just point the way. He walks the way — carrying His cross — with us.

In all the Lents of our lives — and in our lives which are an everlasting Lent — all the times when Christ asks us to deny ourselves, He is beside us. He strives to teach us that great lesson — happiness consists in being emptied of self and being filled with, and fulfilled by, Christ.

Living this kind of lifetime Lent, we are assured that at the end of it — as with all Lents — there is Easter and Resurrection and "joy prepared for us in heaven from all eternity."

46 The Part WE Play

In some Church circles today I often hear the statement that "the Church belongs to the young." I would like to make a small demurrer to that claim. Of course, I pray it does belong to them in the future and that they learn to love and cherish and carry it on as have their ancestors. But, it is not theirs — just yet.

Yes, we care about them and their growth in faith and virtue and devotion. We yearn and we work and we pray in the hope that they will find in the Church all the answers to the troubling questions their world faces them with today. But, prescinding from the workings of the Holy Spirit (not exactly an easy thing to do, by any means) it seems to me that in the practical order, the carrying of the Church forward belongs to the oldsters. It is the burden of us seniors to get the Church from "here" to "there," from one decade to the next, through one crisis or another.

Lent and the Passion of Christ remind us that it was ever thus, right from the beginning. At the time of the Crucifixion, it was Mary and Nicodemus and Joseph of Arimathea who took the battered body of Jesus and washed it, anointed it and wrapped it in its burial shroud. It was they who carried the body of Christ to its final resting place. It was those older people who bore the burden of seeing that the hard and difficult chores were performed to fulfill the total mission of Christ. He was to be buried that he might rise again on the third day.

If, in these days of change, we are ever tempted to think that the Church's parade has passed us by, we may dismiss the temptation summarily. There *wouldn't be* any parade without us and our perseverance, our loyalty, our willingness to accept change. Our wholehearted support — so-

cially, prayerfully, financially and otherwise — is helping, as with Nicodemus and Joseph of Arimathea and Mary, to fulfill the mission of Christ.

It is the magnificent part we are asked to play — and for playing it as magnificently as we do, I am confident our reward will be great in heaven.

The Church someday will "belong" to today's young people.

Pray that, in that day, when they are called upon to play the part we do now, they match our stride and steps.

47 The Stations of the Cross

In the past year I read a fascinating article about a family that was searching for a Catholic church where they felt comfortable worshiping. The family members were not at all happy with their current parish and undertook a Sunday by Sunday visiting of parishes in their city to find one that gave them a sense of piety and devotion and reverence for the Mass and the Eucharist.

I know — I know — some may read that paragraph and shake their heads at these searchers, rating them as too particular or too difficult. The Mass is the Mass, they may say. If it is validly offered, its benefits flow to us no matter what attendant circumstance there may be to disturb us. The parish Mass may not be exactly as we might want it, but that is no reason to be so picky and critical that we have to go touring our home town looking for exactly the liturgy that pleases our taste.

The burden of this reflection is not on whether or not our searchers should be out hunting Sunday services they

find palatable. I might be inclined to rise to their defense if I saw the liturgy they were being subjected to in their home parish. Let's face it, some of these liturgies can be wearying, dismaying, boring. Too much of Father Performer and his lay hyperactivists putting on their Sunday show can be devastating to a person's devotional sense — especially, if we happen to be inclined to the very traditionalist way of priests and people doing things at Sunday Mass.

My interest in this story was about an incident that had nothing to do with Sunday service. In part of the article, the author was describing a couple of the churches he attended and what he found there. In one, he was mystified by seeing the Stations of the Cross draped with gay, almost gaudy banners. In addition to the banners, each station was festooned with artificial flowers.

His curiosity proved too much for him. He went to the pastor of the church and just had to ask what was the symbolism of the decoration about each station. The pastor explained that since Christ had risen, there was no need to keep the solemn, depressing mode so usually attached to the stations. There was no longer a suffering, crucified Christ now, only a risen Savior. He said he wanted his people to know the joy of Christ's Resurrection and not the dismal spirit of Christ suffering and dying. The answer took the author's breath away.

I'm surprised that the man was so surprised. Is there anything in our modern Catholic Church — outside the Rosary — that has fallen on such hard times as devotion to the Stations of the Cross? Where once Lent pivoted on the weekly recitation of the Stations by the parish, the penitential season can now come and go and the devotion is totally ignored among the paraliturgical services held for Lent. If you were to receive a dime for every sermon preached of late that encouraged the "making" of the Stations, it's doubtful

that you'd pick up enough money for a cup of coffee in the local diner.

How tragic that one of the great traditional devotions has fallen on such neglectful times!

It would be an exercise in futility and a waste of time castigating those who have denigrated the importance of the Stations of the Cross. In the development of our spirituality, the devotion should hold the same prominence as it does in the attitude of the Church. And what does the Church think of it? Perhaps no other pious exercise is as heavily indulgenced by the Church through the centuries as the Stations. This gives some small indication, of course, of what the heart and the mind of the Church is concerning this traditional practice.

All the Father Feelgoods in the world may try to hide, neglect, bury the Cross. They may try substituting their vapid preachments on our being a lovers' Church or a resurrection people or whatever else they can concoct. Their efforts will not avail. The Cross was prominent on the first Good Friday — it topped the hill of Calvary. From that day to this it has topped our faith, our lives, our churches. It is the sign by which we conquer, it is the sign under which we are saved. And no less a chosen apostle than St. Paul has written that we "glory in the cross of Christ"!

In this reflection, I urge all to take out of hiding that magnificent devotion, the Stations of the Cross. We need not wait for another Lent to pray them. If we are impeded from getting to church to say the Stations, we may make them at home. They do not have to be prayed all at once. They can be said one at a time, interrupted if need be, and resumed at our convenience until we have completed the fourteen meditations. No special prayers need be offered for each station. Merely a brief meditation on the particular

theme of the station itself. They can be offered in any order, backward or forward.

The point is they are salvific and should have an important place in our spirituality. We should turn to them in trials and stress, pain and hurt, making them help us in carrying the cross Christ said we must carry in imitation of Him. They have a place in our lives.

Pray God that we wake up and give them back their place in our Church.

48   Young of Soul

Whenever Easter and spring break upon our world and herald the excitement of renewal and resurrection for the world, I have found too many seniors very laconic about the arrival of those twin poles of optimistic outlook. Too many seem to go around humming that old George Gershwin tune: "But Not For Me."

I can't resist challenging them by asking: "Why not for you? Why not for us?"

I suppose the negativism comes from feeling that ever-pervading ache in the back or that unrelenting throb in stiff joints. Whatever it is, Sir and Madam Senior just don't see themselves as taking on the friskiness of a teenager as the season, and the feast, of rejuvenation brighten up the landscape. They tend to count their birthdays and opine that "it's great when you're young — but me? — hey! I'm going in the other direction. I'm on the edge of the perpetual winter of life."

How wrong they are!

Certainly, if we want to live IN and BY and FOR the

body with its warp and warts and wrinkles, we can count ourselves old. Certainly, we will not get younger as the years flow by. It is a given of nature that where the body is concerned we can't turn back the clock.

Easter and the celebrating of the resurrection of Christ remind us, however, that we don't live for this body alone. We live for that *spirit*, the soul God gave us, which vivifies us and elevates us to a supernatural life.

At any time of the year or any time of our lives, this spirit can know the joy of spring and the glory of resurrection. No matter what the number of our years, we can be YOUNG OF SOUL. Unlike the body, the soul does not wrinkle or stoop, bend or break. It does not surrender to time because it was made for eternity.

As St. Paul says: "Though our outer nature is being wasted away, our inner nature is being renewed every day" (2 Cor 4:16). The soul can know the joy of renewal any time it is willing to move to God and pray for it. God answers the prayer through the sacraments of Penance and the Eucharist, through the graces and blessing He pours out on us in response to our plea.

I guess we might say that spring is not necessarily a special time of the year for seniors. *Anytime* is special time of the year, if we truly wish it. We don't have to be able to run a country mile to prove it. All that we need to do is to run to Christ who promised that all would be renewed in Him.

49   What of the Others?

Coming to the close of our spiritual reflections, I am reminded of my young priest friend whom I introduced you to in the beginning of these meditations.

One remark of his has persisted with me all through these pages. He said that for those seniors who had not learned to say their prayers, it was too late.

I don't think he meant so mordant a statement. His smart-alecky remark was uttered to make me rise to a challenge and argue with him, which, you can be sure, I did.

As a priest he knew better than that, I asserted. We, of all people, know that it is *never* too late. No priest could believe that and be true to the close following of Christ that the priesthood demands. We, in imitation of our model, the great and first priest, Jesus Christ, are ordained "to call sinners" to repentance. All of us have had our share of deathbed confessions and they have fixed in our heart the knowledge that it is NEVER too late for conversion of heart.

Time upon time, Christ illustrated this fact in His life as we study it in the Gospels. With Magdalen, the Good Thief on the cross, Nicodemus, Joseph of Arimathea, and a host of others of His converts, He declares to all that it is NEVER too late. In His story of the Good Shepherd, He leaves us a telling demonstration that it is NEVER too late.

Certainly, as far as God is concerned it is NEVER too late.

If there is any problem, it has to be with us. We are the ones who delay, who fend Him off, or postpone turning to Him when He calls.

If any of us are guilty of this stalling attitude with God, we should end it today, now. True as it is that for God it is NEVER too late, it could get to the point of being too late for us. It is not God's mercy and love that run out for us, it is time.

My presumption, however, is that those of us who have got this far in our reflections on senior spirituality are not among those who have postponed turning to Christ.

My concern is for those who have not turned to Him; for those who are tepid, indifferent, estranged.

What of that vast horde of seniors out there who never give their spiritual life a thought — the millions who have never developed a sense of the presence of God in their lives? What about all those who have never, as my young priest friend phrased it, "learned to say their prayers"?

If we live among them, in apartments, boarding or nursing homes, neighborhoods, we can show them by our own fervent example the positive benefits of union with God. In faithfulness to our Church and its obligations, in the gracious acceptance of the burdens of old age that God lays upon us, in cheerful service of other seniors who are confined or handicapped, we can demonstrate that by living our lives with and in God, we have chosen the "better way."

If we suspect that people are open to an invitation to come closer to God, we might invite them to accompany us to church. At least, we might invite them to some social function in a parish and let them get the feel of being in a "religious" atmosphere. Simply, if a person who has been away from God seems well-disposed, we should look for an occasion, an opportunity, for them to take that first step back toward reconciliation.

At the very least, we can select someone whom we recognize as a drifter, lacking spiritual anchor, and pray for his or her conversion. That someone can be made "our apostolate."

What happier mission could there be for us than to bring a soul back to God?

What greater gift could we give God for His having taught us to say our prayers than that we help someone else learn to say theirs?

50   John Paul II Speaks to the Elderly

On his Australian trip in 1986, Pope John Paul II gave a beautiful talk to the elderly when he visited Perth. I can think of no better conclusion to our reflections on seniority than having us share some of these inspiring thoughts of our Holy Father.

"Dear Brothers and Sisters in Christ:

"You know that wherever I go, I enjoy being with the young, that they inspire me with their enthusiasm. But I also want you to know that I experience great happiness when I am with the aged. You give me a share in your peace and in the accumulated wisdom of your lives.

"Let us live this moment together in a spirit of thanksgiving to God for the lives he has given us. You can look back on lives rich in memories. Many of you have your children and your children's children to be proud of. Perhaps some of you remember times of pain and the hopes that never quite materialized. But all of us — to use the words of the First Letter of St. John — *Know and believe the love God has for us* (1 Jn 4:16). Yes, God has loved and continues to love each of you in a deep and personal way. If you think back, you will see that your whole life is a story of God's love coming upon you in successive stages. Life itself is a gift of the Father's love, as was your baptism, your Christian faith and the presence of the Holy Spirit down through the years. For all these gifts we sing a hymn of gratitude to God: *Blessed be the Lord who has shown me the wonders of his love* (Ps 31:21).

"While old age brings with it the challenge to look back to the past, it is also a time of responsibility for the *future*. It is an invitation to take a new interest in life, to enter into a new relationship with the world. The elderly do not usually take part in social and political activity, but you still can contri-

bute a great deal in making the world a better place. You have experience to share, wisdom to impart, tolerance to teach, though these are not always evident to younger people. Your words of peace and love are greatly needed in today's society. Above all it is through your life of prayer — at times accompanied by suffering — that you will help bring the redeeming love of Christ to the world.

"May peace be the atmosphere in which you pass your days and may it be firmly established in your souls."

An Interesting Thought

The publication you have just finished reading is part of the apostolic efforts of the Society of St. Paul of the American Province. The Society of St. Paul is an international religious community located in 23 countries, whose particular call and ministry is to bring the message of Christ to all people through the communications media.

Following in the footsteps of their patron, St. Paul the Apostle, priests and brothers blend a life of prayer and technology as writers, editors, marketing directors, graphic designers, bookstore managers, pressmen, sound engineers, etc. in the various fields of the mass media, to announce the message of Jesus.

If you know a young man who might be interested in a religious vocation as a brother or priest and who shows talent and skill in the communications arts, ask him to consider our life and ministry. For more information at no cost or obligation write:

Vocation Office
2187 Victory Blvd.
Staten Island, NY 10314-6603
Telephone: (718) 698-3698